Serving Teens and Adults on
the Autism Spectrum

SERVING TEENS AND ADULTS ON THE AUTISM SPECTRUM

A Guide for Libraries

Carrie Rogers-Whitehead

LIBRARIES UNLIMITED®

An Imprint of ABC-CLIO, LLC

Santa Barbara, California • Denver, Colorado

Copyright © 2020 by Carrie Rogers-Whitehead

Library of Congress Cataloging-in-Publication Data

Names: Rogers-Whitehead, Carrie, 1983– author.
Title: Serving teens and adults on the autism spectrum : a guide for
    libraries / Carrie Rogers-Whitehead.
Description: Santa Barbara, California : Libraries Unlimited, [2020] |
    Includes bibliographical references and index.
Identifiers: LCCN 2020011233 (print) | LCCN 2020011234 (ebook) |
    ISBN 9781440874819 (paperback ; acid-free paper) |
    ISBN 9781440874826 (ebook)
Subjects: LCSH: Libraries and the developmentally disabled. |
    Autism spectrum disorders.
Classification: LCC Z711.92.D48 R64 2020 (print) | LCC Z711.92.D48 (ebook) |
    DDC 027.6/63—dc23
LC record available at https://lccn.loc.gov/2020011233
LC ebook record available at https://lccn.loc.gov/2020011234

ISBN: 978-1-4408-7481-9 (paperback)
    978-1-4408-7482-6 (ebook)

24 23 22 21 20   1 2 3 4 5

This book is also available as an eBook.

Libraries Unlimited
An Imprint of ABC-CLIO, LLC

ABC-CLIO, LLC
147 Castilian Drive
Santa Barbara, California 93117
www.abc-clio.com

This book is printed on acid-free paper (∞)

Manufactured in the United States of America

For "Miss Chris"
aka Chris Kamlowsky
and her tireless service for those with autism, and being a caring friend.

Contents

Preface

This book uses people-first language (also known as person-first language) when speaking about those with autism. People-first language (PFL) puts the individual over their diagnosis. It's a requirement in the American Medical Association's manual of style, and is used in U.S. government institutions on the federal level, such as with the Centers for Disease Control and Prevention.

However, there is another style of language: identity first. Here's an example of how the two languages are used:

> **People-first language:** *Person with autism*
> **Identity-first language:** *Autistic person*

The reader should know that there is controversy between the two styles of languages. An autistic person I interviewed for this book, J, has this to say on the subject:

When people use "person-first language," they say, "You are not your diagnosis! You are so much more than that! Don't let it define you!" But it does define me. Autism is not an accessory I carry around with me, separate from myself. In fact, if you were to try to separate me from it, I would no longer recognize myself. My friends and family would no longer recognize me. I would literally not be the same person.

It affects how I experience the world around me (e.g., the way I hear sounds), the way I navigate through the world, the way I move my body, the way I form and express my thoughts, the way I interpret what's happening around me. It directs my hopes, dreams, fears, and passions. Try taking those things away from yourself, and tell me if you'd still be you.

This is important because when people use PFL, they are implying that autism is a negative thing that I would want to be detached from, to not be "defined by." You have no problem calling me right-handed, even though those aspects don't define me in the slightest. You'd sound silly calling me "an individual with right-handedness." Because there's no stigma about handedness (at least, not anymore!), so you don't feel the need to tiptoe around it or artificially separate me from it.

When I interviewed those with autism for this book, I asked them how they would like to be referred. Some preferred people-first language, others identity-first. If a library staff member is unsure what style to use, just ask the person.

Autism is a spectrum of many abilities, opinions, identities, experiences, and desires. It is difficult to speak for everyone in the spectrum. When writing this book, I kept in mind my audience, librarians. From my experience as a librarian, I would have wanted a book with more suggestions and advice for those with autism that perhaps struggle more with their diagnosis. This book is written in that lens. It focuses more on services and adaptations for those with autism who may struggle. This group on the spectrum may not be able to live unassisted, might be nonverbal, and have multiple conditions that affect their day-to-day life. However, the reader should note that not *all* those with autism are in that situation.

I want the reader to know that I am not autistic and do not speak for that community. I strove in writing this book to feature those voices, the ones who are #actuallyautistic, and their thoughts and stories are throughout the book. If you are working to improve your library services to those with autism, I encourage you to reach out to them.

This book, and the library programs I've done throughout the years, would not exist without the Utah autism community. They guided, advised, introduced, advocated, and helped me. I am in debt to their assistance, and I hope this book can help me pay it forward.

Introduction

Over half a million individuals with autism will become adults by 2027 according to the National Autism Indicators Report (U.S. Department of Health and Human Services, 2017b). More adults are being diagnosed with autism, and those diagnosed as children are growing up. Although teens and adults do not develop autism, diagnostic tools have improved since they were children, which may make their diagnosis come later in life. Children are screened and diagnosed at earlier ages now. Clinicians also have a better understanding of the variability of symptoms and behaviors of autism. Autism is a spectrum and can manifest in widely different ways depending on the individual.

A study from the *American Journal of Medical Genetics* in 2015 found a 331 percent increase in autism diagnosis from 2000 to 2010 from the recategorization of autism diagnosis, and how autism can be marked through other co-occurring illnesses (Polyak et al., 2015). Most of those individuals who had their disorders recategorized by autism were older children, who then subsequently would not have the same level of early intervention as those younger. Early intervention is important for those with autism. It can improve IQ and in some cases can assist children to join mainstream school classes earlier. Treatments can start as early as eighteen months for infants who have a diagnosis (Eldevik et al., 2009).

There is no outbreak of autism, just better awareness and understanding. This leads to a large cohort of older children diagnosed a decade or less ago, now approaching or already reaching adulthood. Service providers are not prepared for this oncoming demographic wave. This growing group of adults will need inclusive housing, medical care, jobs, education, legal assistance, recreational activities, and much more. We also don't fully understand how to integrate this group into employment, schooling, and the larger society. Only about 2 percent of federal and private funding goes into researching how teens with autism can better transition into healthy, functioning adults, according to the U.S. Department of Health and Human Services (U.S. Department of Health and Human Services, 2017b).

Teens and adults with autism spectrum disorder (ASD) have a unique set of needs that many service providers are not trained for. A general practitioner may know how to diagnosis an illness, but not how that illness can interact with ASD. A lawyer may understand the law, but not how that law affects someone who cannot care for themselves. A librarian may know how to create teen programs, but not how to make those programs inclusive for individuals on the spectrum.

Cheryl Smith, parent of Carson, an adult with autism, describes the experience of trying to find help for her son (conversation with the author, May 2019):

> *Carson has Type II diabetes and high blood pressure. With the exception of the Neurobehavior HOME program, I have not found physicians that see adults with autism. Specialists that know anything about autism AND diabetes in the adult world are nonexistent. After he turned 18 and Primary Children's Hospital "broke up" with us, it's been very hard. I can find a diabetes doctor, but they know nothing about autism; that makes it hard to go to the appointment, understand how he might react to the doctor and the meds, get the understanding of how he might to react to shots, finger prick, etc. Autism is the overarching problem which affects all else.*

It is very unlikely that any library education program provides information about serving individuals with autism. A librarian may learn reader's advisory, but not how to ask a nonverbal individual on the spectrum what they like to read. They may learn how to build a website, but not how to make that website adaptable to individuals with disabilities. This is not the failure of library schools; it's impossible to teach everything needed. It's not a failure of medical schools either. Systems and structures take time to change, and the growth of autism diagnoses has outpaced that change. Although autism awareness has certainly grown in the last ten to fifteen years, awareness does not always equal accommodations.

YOUR AVERAGE TEEN OR ADULT WITH AUTISM

What does this oncoming wave of teens and adults look like? Most of them are male, about 75 percent. However, researchers are questioning that percentage. The National Autistic Society in the United Kingdom conducted a survey which found that women and girls are less likely to be diagnosed. Forty-two percent of women were diagnosed with a mental disorder other than autism when they were assessed. There may be many women that need to be recategorized as autism as diagnostic assessments improve (National Autistic Society, n.d.).

Other characteristics of the group of people diagnosed with autism are that they are mostly non-Hispanic white. Over half of autism diagnoses are Caucasian. However, that is not because autism does not affect all racial groups the same. The Centers for Disease Control and Prevention (CDC) has conducted studies that find the rates of autism are almost identical, but despite that, white children are 30 percent more likely to have an autism diagnosis than African Americans (Centers for Disease Control and Prevention, 2019).

In the article "Autism's Race Problem," the writer Carrie Arnold describes the process of diagnosis as a "slog." She writes, "An average of two years passes, regardless of race, between the time parents first recognize issues with their child and when the child receives an autism diagnosis. For minority children, however, that time tends to be significantly longer . . . these children are either left undiagnosed or are misdiagnosed with an adjustment or conduct disorder" (Pacific Standard, 2016).

This lack of diagnoses with minority children relates to another characteristic of the coming wave of adults with autism. This group is typically of a higher socioeconomic class. They are more likely to have a parent with a bachelor's degree and grow up in a two-parent household. These parents have more resources to attain that diagnosis and to get early intervention services. Navigating the system takes more time, energy, and transportation than a single-parent household or one without as much income has. Transportation can be an issue with the various appointments and checkups. Arnold writes, "Getting the proper services for a child often requires detailed knowledge of the inner workings of the school system, a comprehension of the minutiae of laws and regulation, and the time and ability to show up at meetings armed with information" (Pacific Standard, 2016).

Raising children on the spectrum is very expensive. A *JAMA Pediatrics* study found that it cost about $2.4 million dollars to support someone with autism during their life span. The biggest costs as children were educational services and the loss of productivity from parents. An autism diagnosis makes it harder for both parents to work full-time and balance the needs of work and family. As those with autism age, the biggest expenses for families shift to residential care and medical costs. Teens and adults on the spectrum from lower-income families may not have received as many services as those with more money. This can set them behind in school and later in their careers. Unfortunately, treatment and services for autism, particularly for older groups, are not equitable (Buescher et al., 2014).

Teens and adults with autism are typically more severe, often referred to as "low functioning." These individuals typically have a lower IQ and higher needs for supports. Individuals with more severe forms of autism most likely will never mainstream. Those who are minimally verbal or nonverbal will always need additional support and services. They can also experience mental health concerns, partly due to the frustration from not being able to communicate their needs and thoughts.

Research from Boston University finds that about 30 percent of individuals with autism are minimally verbal, or nonverbal. Minimally verbal people may know a few words, while those who are nonverbal may only communicate with hand signs, grunts, or other gestures (Berdik et al., 2014). This book focuses its advice and resource on this group with more needs for services.

In contrast, children with mild autism that is diagnosed early and who have received early intervention services sometimes mainstream from special education to regular classes as they age. The more mild version of autism is often referred to as "high functioning." They do not present as many symptoms, and librarians may not even know they have a diagnosis.

Most individuals with autism have multiple health issues, more than the average population, according to the 2017 National Autism Indicators Report. Those mental health concerns typically increase with age. The report states that six out of ten adults with ASD take medication for behavioral challenges such as depression, anxiety, or psychosis. These adults are also more likely to have self-injurious or disruptive and/or destructive behaviors (Roux et al., 2017).

The outlook for teens and adults with autism can be grim. They suffer from more mental and physical health concerns than their peers. They have less access to services than children with autism. And there is less research and understanding of this group than young children on the autism spectrum (Carpenter, 2015). However, there is increasingly awareness of these service needs in the government and education. Other concerns unique to this population will be explored in more detail in Chapter 1.

THE CLIFF

In special needs the term "the cliff" is used to describe the moment when an individual with autism does not qualify for services (Carpenter, 2015). Cliff is an apt analogy, because the funding stops abruptly, like the land running out before a deep ravine. This is a moment many parents fear and when additional struggles and concerns begin.

The Individuals with Disabilities Education Act (IDEA), created in 1990, provides free public education until age 21. IDEA was reauthorized in 2004, and the U.S. Congress stated their reasoning, which was that "improving educational results for children with disabilities is an essential element of our national policy of ensuring equality of opportunity, full participation, independent living, and economic self-sufficiency for individuals with disabilities." IDEA funds early intervention for infants and toddlers as well as services for K–12 students. It also offers different grants to state agencies, colleges, and other organizations working with individuals with disabilities ("Individuals with Disabilities Education Act," n.d.).

When individuals turn 21, they are said to have fallen off "the cliff." Funding and services rapidly dry up. Under the IDEA Act, students and parents have an IEP, an individualized education program. This program includes a team of specialists and educators, all working together to provide coordinated care and education for the child. With that team and a plan based on the needs of the child, students can better integrate into the school environment and receive the adaptive care they need. Suddenly at 21, that team is gone, and a parent must cobble together a patchwork of specialists and help for their child.

Karla Stoker, mother of Eric Stoker, now an adult with autism, described her experience through the IEP process for the first time.

> I remember it was probably when Eric was in second or third grade. I went with my husband, and when we returned from the meeting he said, "Oh my Gosh, that was so stressful. I need a nap." I don't think they intend it to be stressful, but as a parent you spend a significant amount of time learning where the gaps are and what are the goals.... Coming to terms with maybe seeing that gap growing in some areas is really sobering. You just go "this is so much work, what's going to happen to them?"

There is no federal agency that coordinates developmental disabilities services. Parents must navigate a complex world of local, public, and private services. Funding is mixed as well. With IDEA there is dedicated federal funding, plus additional government grants for service providers. A parent going to a service provider that worked with their 20-year-old may find that the agency provides no services for their now 21-year-old. Without federal funding, many agencies focus their attention on younger people.

Some funding for adults may come from Medicaid and Supplemental Security Income (SSI), but the funding pool is smaller. To qualify for Medicaid, families must be at a certain poverty level and have a qualified medical need. Each state defines the terms of how Medicaid funding is provided, and some families that may qualify in one state may not qualify in another (U.S. Department of Health and Human Services, 2017a).

Even if someone has not yet fallen off the cliff, the amount of services and funding available for teens is less than for younger children. In an article with the Washington Autism Alliance, Catherine Lord, professor at the University of California, Los Angeles, said, "The reality is we don't know much about what the services are that teenagers and young adults are getting" (Washington Autism Alliance & Advocacy, 2018). The IDEA Act does mandate that public schools work with teens on planning next steps, but it is hard to get an estimate of what exactly is occurring. A study, SEED Teen, by the Centers for Disease Control and Prevention, hopes to study adolescents with autism. It was launched in 2018 and goes through 2021 and will hopefully have more data to help parents and practitioners better serve this group. Research studies by the CDC on younger children, however, have been going on for years (Centers for Disease Control and Prevention, 2019).

This cliff can be extremely stressful for families and highlight the lack of services for older individuals on the spectrum. Many parents may need to pay even more out of pocket for services or change their own schedules to make sure their child is cared for. Parents with adult children with autism may also be dealing with their own health issues due to aging. Their ability to provide that care may be diminished. In addition, parents may have other children and aging parents that they also must care for. The lack of funding means less money for respite care for these parents, affecting them physically and mentally.

The cliff affects the whole family, not just the individual with autism. Although there is increased awareness of the need for more services for older individuals with autism, funding is nowhere near enough to provide those services. I first learned about the cliff from parents in my sensory story time. They had children as young as 3 and 4 and were already preparing and ruminating on their children's futures. These parents know that they will outlive their children, and they are concerned about who will care for them when they are gone.

Libraries are in a unique and enviable position to meet some of those needs for older individuals with autism. Libraries are not dependent on IDEA funding; they have other sources. They are also a place with which families are already familiar and which they trust. Later in this book, specific ideas and resources will be discussed for libraries to help deal with the crises and stress caused by the cliff.

CALL TO ACTION FOR LIBRARIES

There is an increasing need for support for this growing population. This oncoming wave will need a network of service providers and people and organizations dedicated to help them transition to and navigate adulthood (Resources and Services for Adults with Autism, 2019). This network must be community based and coordinated. Awareness and research are increasing for this group, but it lags behind the number of diagnoses and requests of need. Currently, there exists a gap, a cliff that many individuals unfortunately fall off.

Libraries have a mission to serve and inform the public and are uniquely suited to help fill that gap. They are already at the heart of the community and coordinate with multiple partners. Libraries have dedicated staff, spaces, resources, programs, and more. Many teens and adults on the spectrum already consider the library a safe space and use their services. Libraries are in a position to step up and serve and make a difference in the lives of more people on the autism spectrum. Not only can libraries help individuals on the autism spectrum, but they can assist the families, friends, and others affected by the diagnosis. Will you help answer the call?

REFERENCES

Berdik, Chris, Jackie Ricciardi, and Devin Hahn. 2014, October 28. "Unlocking Emily's World: The Brink." Boston University. https://www.bu.edu/articles/2014/autism.

Buescher, Ariane, Cidav Zuleyha, Martin Knapp, and David S. Mandell. 2014. "Costs of Autism Spectrum Disorders in the United Kingdom and the United States." *JAMA Pediatrics* 168, no. 8. https://jamanetwork.com/journals/jamapediatrics/fullarticle/1879723.

Carpenter, Siri. 2015, March 23. "For Adults with Autism, a Lack of Support When They Need It Most." *Washington Post*, WP Company. https://www.washingtonpost.com/national/health-science/for-adults-with-autism-a-lack-of-support-when-they-need-it-most/2015/03/23/cd082c64-b396-11e4-854b-a38d13486ba1_story.html.

Centers for Disease Control and Prevention. 2019, August 27. "SEED-Teen." n.d. Centers for Disease Control and Prevention. https://www.cdc.gov/ncbddd/autism/seed-teen.html.

Cottrell, Megan. 2019, April 29. "Aging Out of Sensory Storytime." American Libraries. https://americanlibrariesmagazine.org/2016/04/29/libraries-autism-services-aging-sensory-storytime.

Eldevik, S., R. P. Hastings, J. C. Hughes, E. Jahr, S. Eikeseth, and S. Cross. 2009. "Meta-Analysis of Early Intensive Behavioral Intervention for Children with Autism." *Journal of Clinical Child & Adolescent Psychology* 38: 439–50.

"For Parents of Autistic Children, More Social Support Means Better Health." 2016, April 6. *ScienceDaily*. https://www.sciencedaily.com/releases/2016/04/160406124631.htm.

"Individuals with Disabilities Education Act (IDEA)." n.d. Individuals with Disabilities Education Act. Accessed May 13, 2019. https://sites.ed.gov/idea.

National Autistic Society. "How Do Women and Girls Experience Autism?" n.d. Accessed June 16, 2019. https://www.autism.org.uk/about/what-is/gender/stories.aspx.

"New on ADA.gov." n.d. ADA.gov homepage. Americans with Disabilities Act. Accessed May 16, 2019. https://ada.gov.

Pacific Standard. 2016, May 25. "Autism's Race Problem." Pacific Standard. https://psmag.com/news/autisms-race-problem.

Polyak, Andrew, Richard M. Kubina, and Santhosh Girirajan. 2015. "Comorbidity of Intellectual Disability Confounds Ascertainment of Autism: Implications for Genetic Diagnosis." *American Journal of Medical Genetics Part B: Neuropsychiatric Genetics* 168, no. 7: 600–608. https://doi.org/10.1002/ajmg.b.32338.

"Resources and Services for Adults with Autism." n.d. Resources and Services for Adults with Autism. Autism Speaks. Accessed May 16, 2019. https://www.autismspeaks.org/adults-autism.

Roux, Anne M., Jessica E. Rast, Kristy A. Anderson, and Paul T. Shattuck. 2017. *National Autism Indicators Report: Developmental Disability Services and Outcomes in Adulthood*. Philadelphia: Life Course Outcomes Program, A. J. Drexel Autism Institute, Drexel University.

Roux, Anne M., P. T. Shattuck, B. P. Cooper, K. A. Anderson, M. Wagner, and S. C. Narendorf. 2013. "Postsecondary Employment Experiences among Young

Adults with an Autism Spectrum Disorder." *Journal of the American Academy of Child and Adolescent Psychiatry* 52, no. 9: 931–39.

U.S. Department of Health and Human Services. 2017a. "Who Is Eligible for Medicaid?" HHS.gov. https://www.hhs.gov/answers/medicare-and-medicaid/who-is-eligible-for-medicaid/index.html.

U.S. Department of Health and Human Services. 2017b. "Report to Congress: Young Adults and Transitioning Youth with Autism Spectrum Disorder." https://www.hhs.gov/sites/default/files/2017AutismReport.pdf.

Washington Autism Alliance & Advocacy. 2018, October 1. "Autism Prevalence Program Expands to Include Teenagers." https://www.washingtonautismadvocacy.org/updates/tag/funding.

What Is Autism?

Autism spectrum disorder (ASD), often just referred to as autism, is a developmental disorder that manifests early in life. It impairs communication and can cause difficulties in creating and maintaining relationships. ASD can also affect a broad range of characteristics: intelligence, motor skills, IQ, influence repetitive behaviors, and more. There's a common phrase in the autism community that if you've met one person with autism, you've met one person with autism. This means that the condition is wide-ranging with different effects for each individual.

One defining characteristic of autism is social isolation. The word *autism* originates from the Greek word "autos," which means "self." Those with autism may be isolated because of lack of verbal communication, having limited interests, preference for solitude, or isolation from peers or family who do not understand them (Alli, n.d.).

This chapter summarizes the latest claims, controversies, and characteristics of ASD. It also lays out the differences between children, adolescents, and adults with autism.

HISTORY OF AUTISM

Autism has always existed, but not as a specific diagnosis with a name. The first person to formally describe the symptoms of autism was Eugen Bleuler in 1911. Bleuler saw those symptoms related to schizophrenia. It wasn't until the 1940s and 1950s that researchers started using the term *autism* and as something separate and distinct.

Unfortunately, early treatments for autism were grounded in misunderstandings and lack of research. The term *refrigerator mother* was used in 1950 to describe mothers and parents of children diagnosed with autism or schizophrenia. Mothers were blamed for being too cold or rigid with their children, causing the disorder. In the 1960s and 1970s treatments for autism included electric shock therapy, medications such as LSD, and behavioral change techniques focused on pain and punishment. As the understanding of autism and mental health in general increased, positive behavioral therapy was used as well as an increased focus on early learning and the environment of the individuals with ASD. Today, the main treatments of autism are behavioral and language therapy. Other treatments such as special diets and physical therapy are also used. And while researchers are still studying the origins and causes of autism, it's clear that mothers are not to blame.

Changes in Autism Diagnoses through the Years

The *Diagnostic and Statistical Manual* (DSM) is the ultimate authority on psychiatric conditions and treatment in the United States. The changes in this manual toward ASD reflect the increasing understanding and research into the condition. Autism first appeared in the third edition of the DSM in 1980 under pervasive developmental disorder (PDD). After more information and diagnoses accumulated, the next edition of the DSM—the DSM-IV—was updated and added to the definition of autism in 1994 (Volkmar and Reichow, 2013).

This updated definition added three new disorders: childhood disintegrative disorder, Asperger's disorder, and Rett's disorder. Of those three, Asperger syndrome is the most well known. The disorder is named after Hans Asperger, an Austrian pediatrician who studied children who displayed the symptoms. His observations and research were published in *Autistic Psychopathy in Childhood* in 1944. Those who were diagnosed with Asperger's had less severe symptoms than autism. They may have trouble communicating but have normal intelligence.

Classic autism, defined by another Austrian researcher, Leo Kanner, has differing symptoms. Compared to individuals diagnosed with Asperger syndrome, they have more severe communication difficulties, are sometimes nonverbal, and typically have lower intelligence (Kanner, 1943).

The DSM-V, released in 2013, brought the two diagnoses, Asperger syndrome and autism, together. Instead of including subtypes under PDD, all variations of autism were brought under ASD. Rett's disorder and childhood disintegrative disorder were dropped. This move still remains controversial to some, who feel that there should be separate diagnoses or that the one diagnosis does not accurately describe the symptoms. There is debate on how this diagnosis should be applied in practice, and what services an individual under the umbrella of autism should receive (Volkmar and Reichow, 2013).

Those formerly diagnosed with Asperger syndrome (AS) may be labeled with high-functioning autism (HFA). Although this term is not in the DSM, it commonly refers to those with autism with IQs higher than 70.

A meta-analysis in 2019 from the *Journal of Autism and Developmental Disorders* summarizes some of the discussion on this controversy. "Since AS and HFA are both characterized by a normal cognitive functioning, there has been considerable debate over whether AS and HFA are distinct conditions, suggesting different etiological and neurobiological mechanism, or share a similar underlying neuropsychological functioning and should therefore be regarded as variants of a single disorder" (Giambattista et al., 2018).

The article continues: "Ultimately, the unsolved confusion in defining AS criteria and the clinical overlap between HFA and AS led to its merging into one unifying category, on the assumption that they cannot be reliably differentiated from one another." By combining the categories, some individuals lost their diagnoses. Studies summarized in the 2019 *Journal of Autism and Developmental Disorders* find that about 92 percent of those with Asperger's kept their diagnosis of autism in the DSM-V. There was great fear from parents and from patients who had milder symptoms that they would lose their diagnosis, and thus their access to services. However, follow-up research found that the majority of those who had a diagnosis in the DSM-IV kept theirs in the DSM-V, although it may have been under a different name (Giambattista et al., 2018).

These changes in understanding of ASD may mean that many individuals may not receive an autism diagnosis until adulthood. Anna Decker Smyth (2019) was diagnosed as an adult with autism and describes her experience.

When I was first diagnosed I had mixed emotions. Mostly it was a relief to finally have a way to conceptualize and explain why I am the way I am. It removed a lot of shame and confusion from my mind and helped me feel more at home in my skin. At the same time, some new confusion arose—what do I do with this new information? Do I need to make a public announcement? How do I handle the stigma associated with autism and the relative ignorance most people have about ASD? So far I've kept my diagnosis mostly to myself as I'm still assimilating it into my experience of me and my interactions with the world, but simply having the diagnosis has helped me greatly in navigating my world more skillfully and without apology.

Librarians should take care to respect an autism diagnosis and keep that information private. As Smyth said, the diagnosis can come with stigmas and stereotypes. Libraries can provide valuable information for those who have just received a diagnosis and want to understand themselves.

PDD-NOS AND SCD

SCD stands for social communications disorder. This is a diagnosis that some under the DSM-IV who had Asperger's may have received. SCD is not considered under the umbrella of ASD but is considered a separate communications disorder. Thus, some adults with autism may have lost their diagnoses in the DSM-V and now have the label of SCD.

PDD-NOS stands for pervasive developmental disorder not otherwise specified. It is considered atypical autism and usually a milder form of the disorder. In the DSM-IV PDD was the general category under which autism diagnoses fell. PDD vanished when the next edition, the DSM-V, appeared. Despite it no longer being in the DSM, many individuals and caregivers still use the term.

PDD-NOS and Asperger syndrome are not recognized clinically in the United States. However, they can be found in the International Statistical Classification of Diseases and Related Health Problems (ICD) issued by the World Health Organization. Many teens and adults with autism have come to identify themselves with these labels, despite what the mental health community decides. Let the individual decide with what term they would like to be identified.

CAUSES OF AUTISM

Autism is a multifaceted complex disorder. There is not one cause, although researchers are learning more about the genetics attributing to this diagnosis. It's estimated in the 2018 *Handbook of Clinical Neurology* that over 1,000 genes are potential contributors to the disorder (Ramaswami and Geschwind, 2018). New research is looking into the role of epigenetics. Epigenetics refers to how heritable genes may change their activity or expression beyond alterations in the DNA sequence. These epigenetic changes can happen with mutations, from cancer, effects of chemicals in the womb, X chromosome in activation, certain diets, and more. An individual may possess multiple genes contributing to autism, but until those genes are "turned on" or "activated" through epigenetic processes, they may never manifest any of the symptoms.

A literature review in 2015 out of the *Frontiers in Neurology* writes, "Going beyond genetic associations, alterations in other cellular processes have begun to be found in ASD. Studying changes to physiology, gene expression, and the epigenetic states that contribute to ASD phenotype along with genetics, has begun to broaden our understanding of ASD and will eventually, in combination, lead to better methods of diagnosis, prognosis and even treatment of ASD" (Loke et al., 2015).

Autism runs in families, and there are risk factors found in parents that make it more likely to have a child with autism. Some of these risk factors are advanced ages of the mother or father. Another is exposure to certain drugs or chemicals during pregnancy. What is clear is autism is not caused by parental treatment, but by a complex mix of genetics and chemicals that happened before that child was born. It is also very clear that vaccines do not cause autism.

Comorbidity in Autism

Medical conditions that exist simultaneously and often independently of another condition are called comorbid. For example, a common comorbid condition is heart disease with high blood pressure. When referring to the additional condition, a medical professional may use the word *comorbidity* as, for example, heart disease has a high likelihood of comorbidity with high blood pressure. This does not mean that heart disease caused high blood pressure or vice versa, but it is a possibility.

Autism has a high comorbidity with several conditions including intellectual disability, epilepsy, anxiety, high blood pressure, genetic disorders, attention-deficit hyperactivity disorder, sleep disorders, depression, obesity, and more. Autism is typically the primary diagnosis, but caregivers and medical professionals must treat all comorbid conditions. If a treatment for autism includes only addressing speech issues, but does not help the patient sleep better, the patient may have worse outcomes (Polyak et al., 2015).

One of the most common comorbid conditions is anxiety. Studies have found that up to 84 percent of young people with autism suffer from anxiety. In a busy environment like a library with lots of noise, people, and social situations, this comorbidity may become a troubling issue to an individual with autism (White et al., 2009).

Diagnoses and treating symptoms with comorbid conditions are difficult. A 2015 study from the *American Journal of Medical Genetics* (AJMG) found that "while recent studies suggest a converging role for genetic factors towards risk for . . . disorders including autism, intellectual disability, and epilepsy, current estimates of autism prevalence fail to take into account the impact of these disorders on autism diagnosis." This study found that after analyzing enrollment data of over six million children between 2000 and 2010, they found a 331 percent increase of autism. This suggests that other diagnoses, particularly intellectual disability, were being recategorized as autism. Although these diagnostic tools can help individuals find the best treatment for their conditions, there is a risk of misdiagnosis. One condition can mask another (Polyak et al., 2015).

Better diagnostic tools and treatments are needed. The researchers from the AJMG study recommend "our results suggest that current ascertainment practices are based on a single facet of autism-specific clinical features and do not consider associated comorbidities that may confound diagnosis. . . . deep molecular genetic analyses are necessary to completely understand the cause of this complex disorder" (Polyak et al., 2015).

When working with individuals with autism, understand that they may have multiple diagnoses, each with their own unique set of symptoms. By only addressing the autism, medical professionals, caseworkers, and caregivers may not provide the level of care truly needed.

DIFFERENCES BETWEEN CHILDREN AND ADULTS WITH AUTISM

Children and adults manifest autism differently. The stereotypical "classic" autism traits that people may imagine when they think of autism are less likely to be found in older people. This can make it harder to identify individuals with autism in the library. They look like everyone else, and they may act like all the other library patrons as well. This does not mean that internally they are the same.

All children are learning to regulate their emotions and feelings. For example, a toddler is much more likely to fling themselves on the floor and cry when they are upset, than a 10-year-old. The 10-year-old learned over time that there are appropriate and better ways to express feelings. The 10-year-old also has developed more verbal abilities so that they can tell someone they are upset, rather than demonstrate that feeling by pounding on the ground.

Like neurotypical children, young people with autism also learn over time how to better express and articulate their feelings. They learn to reflect and think, rather than react. When a 5-year-old with autism experiences a strong aversion to something like a food, they may simply push that food out of the way or say, "I hate this." A 15-year-old may have the same aversion to that food, but they will have learned that pushing that food out of the way may affect others, and they may simply say, "Thank you. But I am not interested." Children learn social norms, etiquette, and expected behaviors as they age.

Self-stimulation, also referred to as "stimming," is repeating movements, sounds, objects, and more to self-regulate and calm themselves. They may be over- or understimulated in their environment, so they act out to return to some kind of equilibrium. We all self-regulate. When you are nervous, you may chew your nails or twirl your hair. The difference between someone neurotypically stimming and someone with autism is just the type and degree of stimming. Someone without autism may tap a pencil on their desk, but someone with autism may tap their pencil louder and longer. Sometimes those with autism engage in injurious stimming, biting, pinching, and self-harm.

Older individuals with autism have typically learned more appropriate outlets and behaviors for when they need to calm themselves. Occupational therapy and applied behavioral analysis (ABA) assist with this. Over time school, social norms, and real-life experiences help those with autism learn to regulate their feelings in a more appropriate and less noticeable manner.

Teens and adults with autism have also learned over time what is expected of them in a conversation. They learn that conversation goes two ways, that there are certain niceties or small talk to engage in. Therapies and schooling focus on the back and forth of communication and role play with their students' ways to better empathize and talk. This process is long and never ending, even for those without autism. We continuously learn to communicate in our lives. Those with autism who are older and not nonverbal are more likely to speak in a way more familiar. They may make more eye contact, respond more quickly, ask more questions, and use polite terms like *please* and *thank you.*

Even though teens and adults with autism are more likely to have learned these skills through life experiences and schooling, many cannot mainstream. There is a wide range of abilities on the spectrum. A young child who is high functioning, who perhaps previously had an Asperger's diagnosis, may be in regular classes with their peers and have stopped most therapy. You may not know they have autism at all unless they tell you. On the other extreme of the spectrum, a teen with autism may stand out more than their peers. While this teen with autism did learn skills in occupational therapy and at home, his or her peers also progressed. The gap between abilities appears starker at age 13 than 3. A teen or adult with autism may be simultaneously easier to notice, and harder to identify. That diagnosis that happened at age 3 may become less of a concern or a big liability as that individual ages.

There are other differences between younger and older individuals with ASD. The largest differences are summarized in Table 1.1.

In addition to biological, social, and emotional gaps between age groups, there is a chasm between services and funding. Cheryl Smith (2019), former president of the Autism Council of Utah and mother of an adult with autism,

TABLE 1.1. Differences between Younger and Older Individuals with Autism Spectrum Disorder

Children with Autism	Teens and Adults with Autism
Restricted interests (e.g., Thomas the Train Engine)	Restricted interests but more age appropriate (e.g., computer hardware)
Struggling to both identify and express emotional states	Alexithymia—struggling with identifying one's own emotional states and others
Less likely to engage in eye contact	More likely to be affected by mood disorders and anxiety
Decreased verbal ability	Typically more verbal abilities and have learned "scripts" to communicate
More likely to engage in repetitive behaviors like flapping, twitching, humming, stimming, etc.	Less likely to demonstrate overt movements related to self-regulation/stimulation as children.

said, "The biggest gap I am aware of currently is the need for adult services. There are many providers for young children, insurance and Medicaid coverage and training for parents. When the child with autism becomes an adult, services are sparse."

Early intervention is critically important to help a child adapt and mainstream. But many will not mainstream and need services their entire lives. The gap in services for children versus those of teens and adults will be covered in more detail later in this book.

SEX AND AUTISM

In addition to autism presenting differently between older and younger individuals, there are also differences between sexes (see Table 1.2). Many autism studies and diagnostic tools were created and focused on men, and thus women are not as well represented (Deweerdt, 2014). Smyth (2019), a woman with autism, said, "What we're learning is that females present very differently and most clinicians aren't well trained in understanding the gender differences among autists. It is quite likely that if I were male my behaviors and experience of autism would be very different and perhaps I would have gotten a diagnosis sooner."

Librarians should remember that these differences are generalities and do not apply to everyone. "There's a reason we use the word 'spectrum' to describe autism. It's important to see each individual with autism for who they are, rather than making assumptions," Smyth said.

TABLE 1.2. Differences between Females and Males with Autism

Female	Male
Autism in women is less researched and understood	Autism in men is more researched and understood
Harder to diagnose	Easier to diagnose
More likely to mask or camouflage their symptoms	Less likely to mask or camouflage their symptoms
Less likely to be socially isolated	More likely to be socially isolated than women
Tend to be more severely affected	Less severely affected than women
Less likely to have repetitive movements like hand flapping, stimming, etc.	More likely to demonstrate repetitive movements like hand flapping, stimming, etc.
Their interests are less restricted (e.g., an interest in pop music)	Their interests are more restricted (e.g., an interest in old coins)

Puberty

Puberty is a tough time for everyone. Bodies are going through rapid changes with hormonal highs and lows. The hypothalamus stimulates the pituitary gland to release a flood of hormones called gonadotropins all through the body. These chemical messages stimulate the production of androgen and estrogen. Like in toddlerhood, adolescents are going through an intense period of brain changes and construction. This is to encourage them to take the next step in their development, but as any parent with a toddler or teenager knows, it can cause upheavals in the lives of those around them.

Freddy and Sarah Brown, authors of *When Young People with Intellectual Disabilities and Autism Hit Puberty: A Parents' Q&A Guide to Health, Sexuality and Relationships*, write, "Children with intellectual disabilities face additional challenges that stem from their increased difficulties in understanding what is happening and how they are feeling. To help them through this period of their life they are likely to need extra support and patience as they learn the skills they need to express their emerging sexuality and make healthy choices" (Brown and Brown, 2016).

Puberty affects not only parents and caregivers but others in the individual's orbit. Any librarian who works with teenagers can see firsthand the potential effects of puberty: arguing, the smell of sweat, dating relationships, mood changes in regular patrons, and much more.

As a teen librarian it would sometimes feel like some of my regulars had multiple personalities. One day I would be greeted with a sunny "Hello!" and the next a sullen glare. Part of my time after school was spent moderating feelings and fights. Hygiene was an issue as these growing bodies changed, and a male colleague had to have private chats about deodorant and cologne. One year the issues with cologne, particularly Axe body spray, became a health hazard. The teens would spray so much it was causing other patrons to cough and their eyes to water. Axe body spray had to be banned from the premises.

Puberty is hard. I recognized that in my patrons and did my best to have patience and understanding as they dealt with changes thrust on them by their hormones. In addition, libraries will need to reinforce some boundaries and may potentially have some hard conversations.

"Adolescence is a difficult time for all children . . . For children with intellectual disabilities, the challenges will be all the greater," said Freddy and Sarah Brown. "The nature of their intellectual difficulties mean they will struggle to understand what is happening to their bodies and to communicate their needs" (Brown and Brown, 2016).

Libraries can help families and these children as they navigate puberty. Planned Parenthood provides free resources and classes that may be of interest to libraries. They provide education in such topics as abstinence and birth control education, parent education, safer sex, STDs, and more. Additionally, local nonprofits, health departments, or government agencies may be able to come to libraries to talk about maturation and sexual health ("Patient Education," n.d.).

Unfortunately, this lack of awareness and bodily change can have negative repercussions for individuals with autism and for providers. For example, one may not understand privacy and masturbate in public when they feel the need. This can be a particularly trying issue for libraries, which are public spaces to minors. In their book the Browns write about concerns with the valid desire and need for these individuals to date. "They may want to have a romantic relationship with someone and instead of asking them on a date, they tease or grope them." Libraries should have no-tolerance policies on sexual assault, but this can be harder to enforce with individuals who may not fully understand the policies, how to communicate, and are struggling to understand their changing body. "Learning socially acceptable ways to express their sexuality and communicate what they want is a critical skill, which they may struggle to learn. Or they may never be able to learn these skills and require permanent support with this aspect of who they are" (Brown and Brown, 2016).

Librarians should make sure that if there needs to be rule enforcement with individuals who expose themselves or unknowingly harass other patrons, then that communication needs to go through the caregiver. Communicating policies with a teen or adult with autism who struggles to speak or is nonverbal is not effective. Hopefully, an individual who struggles with privacy and boundaries has a caregiver with them. If not, libraries may have to resort to calling social services.

This is a difficult position for librarians, who want to be empathetic to special needs, but also want to respect the needs of others in their space. Policies and rules should be created with compassion and understanding for both individuals with disabilities and others who are sharing the same space. Librarians must work to protect both sides. More information on crafting library policy will be addressed in Chapter 3.

Adults with Autism

The years are short from when puberty hits and adulthood begins. Although the U.S. educational system may recognize that someone with severe autism may need until 21 to graduate from high school, the rest of governmental structures and systems may not. Although an individual with autism may physically be an adult, cognitively they are not. This unique situation, where the brains and bodies differ in age, will be explored throughout this book.

Legally, adults with autism are treated like adults. This means they can marry and have children. This also means that they are culpable and responsible for laws they may not understand, or potential crimes they did not intentionally commit. This also means they may be subject to library policies created for those with the mental understanding of adults.

MARRIAGE AND DISABILITY

Young adults with disabilities have the same legal right to relationships, sex, and marriage as others. However, there are particular challenges and concerns in these situations. One is financial; Social Security Disability benefits are not available to adults who are married. This marriage penalty can also affect other public benefits like Medicaid by combining two incomes.

Legally, when a marriage occurs, the spouse is named as the primary agent, which includes having power of attorney and making financial and medical decisions. If the spouse of an individual with intellectual disabilities also shares cognitive impairments, these big decisions may be made without a full understanding.

This marriage penalty has detractors and has attracted controversy. Disability rights advocate Dominick Evans wrote on this topic for the Center for Disability Rights:

> People with disabilities need access to services. The exorbitant cost of living with a disability makes it impossible to turn those services down. All of the services I mentioned previously, SSI, Medicaid, SSDI/Medicare, Section 8, Food Stamps, and welfare are impacted, and typically lost, if the person on these programs gets married. That needs to change. Not every person with a disability can have a job, but when we can, we need to be able to make a living wage, as well as have the ability to get married while keeping our healthcare services. (Evans, n.d.)

Adulthood also means that parents and caregivers may have less control, both legally and physically. Cheryl Smith (2019), mother of Carson, an adult with autism, said,

> *I once heard a man say his biggest wish was to live one day longer than his disabled son. The ultimate dread for us, and for every parent of a special needs adult, is no one will love and take care of them like we do. Who will care for him when we're gone? Where will his safe shelter be? Who will be his community? . . . I can't die until I've created a community for my boy where he is safe and happy.*

Teens and adults are with us and need that transition and safe space. Libraries can be part of their community.

REFERENCES

Alli, Renee A. n.d. "What Does the Word 'Autism' Mean?" WebMD. Accessed February 3, 2019. https://www.webmd.com/brain/autism/what-does-autism-mean#1.

Brown, Freddy J., and Sarah Brown. 2016. *When Young People with Intellectual Disabilities and Autism Hit Puberty: A Parents' Q&A Guide to Health, Sexuality and Relationships.* London: Jessica Kingsley.

Deweerdt, Sarah. 2014, March 27. "Autism Characteristics Differ by Gender, Studies Find." *Spectrum News.* https://www.spectrumnews.org/news/autism-characteristics-differ-by-gender-studies-find.

Evans, Dominick. n.d. "Center for Disability Rights." Marriage Equality—Center for Disability Rights. Accessed June 24, 2019. http://cdrnys.org/blog/disability-dialogue/the-disability-dialogue-marriage-equality.

Giambattista, Concetta De, Patrizia Ventura, Paolo Trerotoli, Mariella Margari, Roberto Palumbi, and Lucia Margari. 2018. "Subtyping the Autism Spectrum Disorder: Comparison of Children with High Functioning Autism and Asperger Syndrome." *Journal of Autism and Developmental Disorders* 49, no. 1: 138–50. https://doi.org/10.1007/s10803-018-3689-4.

Kanner, Leo. 1943. "Autistic Disturbances of Affective Contact." *Nervous Child* 2: 217–50.

Loke, Yuk Jing, Anthony John Hannan, and Jeffrey Mark Craig. 2015. "The Role of Epigenetic Change in Autism Spectrum Disorders." *Frontiers in Neurology.* https://doi.org/10.3389/fneur.2015.00107.

"Patient Education." n.d. Planned Parenthood. Accessed June 22, 2019. https://www.plannedparenthood.org/get-care/our-services/patient-education.

Polyak, Andrew, Richard M. Kubina, and Santhosh Girirajan. 2015. "Comorbidity of Intellectual Disability Confounds Ascertainment of Autism: Implications for Genetic Diagnosis." *American Journal of Medical Genetics Part B: Neuropsychiatric Genetics* 168, no. 7: 600–608. https://doi.org/10.1002/ajmg.b.32338.

Ramaswami, Gokul, and Daniel H. Geschwind. 2018. "Genetics of Autism Spectrum Disorder." *Neurogenetics, Part 1 Handbook of Clinical Neurology,* 321–29. https://doi.org/10.1016/b978-0-444-63233-3.00021-x.

Smith, Cheryl. 2019, May. Conversation with author.

Smyth, Anna Decker. 2019, July. Conversation with author.

Volkmar, Fred R, and Brian Reichow. 2013. "Autism in DSM-5: Progress and Challenges." *Molecular Autism* 4, no. 1: 13. https://doi.org/10.1186/2040-2392-4-13.

White, Susan W., Donald Oswald, Thomas Ollendick, and Lawrence Scahill. 2009. "Anxiety in Children and Adolescents with Autism Spectrum Disorders." *Clinical Psychology Review* 29, no. 3: 216–29. doi:10.1016/j.cpr.2009.01.003. PMC 2692135. PMID 19223098.

2

The Needs and Challenges of Those with Autism Spectrum Disorder

Years ago, I toured special education classrooms with an educator. This elementary school had a separate wing with a dedicated staff to help children with disabilities learn and mainstream with their peers. On the tour of these brightly decorated classrooms I asked this educator what they focused on with their students. As we watched the children work at their desks, this educator told me that they narrowed down their focus to three soft skills: teamwork, transitions, and social skills. Those three skills were vital not just for the classroom but to prepare them for what lay beyond school. Their lessons, classroom structure, and schedule were based around those three skills.

After the tour I thought a lot about what she had said and began to incorporate teaching those skills in my sensory programming. I realized I was already doing some of it, but not deliberately. After realizing the significance of those elements, I emphasized them more with my structure, activities, and most importantly, a shift in mind-set.

Those three skills are useful to any population, but as it is explained in this chapter, they're particularly helpful to those with autism. This chapter outlines strategies, program ideas, and the reasons we should think about teamwork, transitions, and social skills when developing any service or program for patrons with autism.

TEAMWORK

Working with others is a vital skill for anyone. In any classroom or career you have to interact with others. For many, this skill comes easily. Teamwork can determine the difference between success and failure in life. Those with autism may struggle in group-based activities. They may not have a friend on the playground, or they may be excluded from peers. In conversation they may stand apart, not knowing what to say. In particular, those on the autism spectrum may find it difficult to be full participating team members.

In the article "Teaching Teamwork to Adolescents with Autism: The Cooperative Use of Activity Schedules," the authors state, "Due to unique learning and behavioral challenges, teaching individuals with autism to work in groups often requires systematic and explicit programming. Additionally, many students with autism have participated in intensive educational programming in which the teacher to student ratio is one-to-one. Individuals who have spent years learning in this instructional format may require assistance from staff members and caretakers to initiate and complete activities and make transitions between them" (White et al., 2011).

Those with autism typically are in smaller classrooms and not as exposed to their peers. They are surrounded by adults: therapists, teachers, parents, speech pathologists, and more. Their parents and caregivers may have been concerned about taking them to children's birthday parties, events, kid-friendly establishments, and more because of fear of behavioral outbursts. Cumulatively, this lack of experience spread out over the years may leave adolescents and adults with autism unprepared for groups of people their own age.

Libraries are an ideal place to encourage teamwork. They are a space for people who are different ages, abilities, backgrounds, and more. They bring people together. And library programs are set up for groups and larger audiences.

Practices to Encourage Teamwork

As detailed in the *Journal of Behavior Analysis in Practice,* in 2011 researchers paired teens with autism who had low levels of functioning together. They were provided picture schedules to perform certain tasks around the school like cleaning the office or the kitchen. They were taught by the experimenters how to perform the tasks before beginning (White et al., 2011).

Working cooperatively was difficult for these teens. Some of the participants in the study were found to repeat tasks. "For example, in one observation, Mike dusted the island and then Sam re-dusted the island," the article states. But with the picture schedule and explicit directions, the participants were able to work together on those tasks and cut down on the time to complete them. Librarians wanting to encourage teamwork should implement some of these recommendations by the researchers:

- Make sure that participants can complete the task individually, before putting them in a group.
- If the task has lots of steps or is very complicated, consider making two picture schedules.
- Consider printing out the schedules and encouraging the participants to cross out the task before they begin to work on it. (White et al., 2011)

Encouraging teamwork is an important skill for transitioning to adult-hood, schooling, or a career. Workplaces require a lot of teamwork, some-times virtually. If an individual with autism is living independently, they may have roommates or be in a group home where they have to interact, share, and coordinate with other people.

More Teamwork Tips

Here are some other tips to encourage teamwork in library programs:

- *Technology.* When using technology like a tablet in a program, make the participants share a device. By sharing, teamwork is encouraged. By assigning multiple people on a device, this can prevent someone from isolating themselves with the device at the program. The use of technology with individuals with autism and some teamwork-related tech activities will be described more in Chapter 8.
- *Games.* Games, or even gamifying activities, naturally encourage teamwork. Consider dividing your group into two, having them pick a side on a topic like a favorite character, and having them debate their interests to the group. More specific games and gamifying strategies will be covered in Chapters 4 and 6.
- *Program layout.* By moving chairs and tables around the room strategically, you can encourage more teamwork and group participation. Gather chairs in a circle where participants have to face each other. Put tables in a configuration to block off certain areas of the room and funnel people toward one space. Don't put out too many tables and chairs; give participants only a few options so that they have to sit near each other.
- *Presorting.* As participants enter the room, give them a name tag or sticker or some kind of designation to pair them with others. For example, for an anime club sort people by Team Shonen or Team Shojo. Other options would be Left Team and Right Team, and sort people on different seating in the room. There are many different options, and by giving someone a team, you give them a tribe and community. They can have a built-in group of people to talk to and work with.
- *Dealing with discomfort.* Librarians may find resistance to encouraging teamwork. One way to overcome this resistance is by starting small. It may take some time for a patron with autism to feel comfortable working directly with another. Ask them to sit near another person; they do not have to talk to them. Have them at the table, sitting across from another. Prompt them both with open-ended questions. Have them share supplies. Coax the participants slowly into interactions and then move to teamwork.

Each year in my sensory group I have a superhero activity. As the partici-pants came into the room, they were given a superhero name generated by a website. This presorting put them in a positive mind-set and let them

PHOTO 2.1. Eric Hall at Superhero Sensory Day.

understand that they were surrounded by other superheroes. After sorting, I would engage the group in a teamwork activity. Hidden around the room were villains, copies of popular villains in the superhero universe printed and laminated. Since the group was now a superhero fighting team, they had to work together to defeat the villains. The best way to encourage teamwork is to have the participants not even realize you're doing it. The room can get busy in these superhero programs, as shown in Photo 2.1.

SAMPLE PROGRAM IDEA THAT INCORPORATES TEAMWORK: CUP STACKING

Cup stacking is what it sounds like—stacking and unstacking cups in various configurations. Cup stacking is not just an activity but a sport. The World Sport Stacking Association (WSSA) is the professional organization that governs the sport, and they have regional, national, and worldwide competitions. Participants must stack cups in specific patterns as fast as they can. This seemingly simple activity can encourage teamwork, motor skills, social skills, balance, and more.

Materials:

- Cups, at least one hundred

  Note: There are specialized cups in stacking; you certainly would not want to use glass cups! These cups are plastic, smooth, and can fit easily in a hand. They also have holes in the top to allow less air resistance. The WSSA sells sport stacking cups for three dollars each. There are other options for cups that are cheaper. However, if you buy plastic cups elsewhere, you will want to puncture holes in the bottom.

- Large space for movement

Instructions:

Activity with a large group

1. Find a large space in the room and put out all the cups in that space.
2. Instruct the participants that they are to make as tall a pyramid as possible. They have to use all the cups. There cannot be multiple pyramids, only one.
3. Watch and encourage.

Activity with small groups

1. Divide the program participants in small groups of two or three people.
2. Give each small group a selection of cups. Each group has an equal number of cups.
3. Instruct the participants to work in small groups to make a cup tower, as tall as they are able. This means stacking cups so that they are inverted, the bottoms of the cups against each other and stacked in one tall structure. This activity requires more balance and patience than creating one large pyramid.
4. Provide a certain amount of time for the towers. Give a reminder when there is a minute to go. When the time runs out, all students must step away from their tower.
5. The winner of this activity is the group with the tallest tower that can stand unsupported.

Optional Activities:

There are many other types of activities that can be done with sport stacking.

- *World Sport Stacking Association activities.* On the WSSA website there are free instructor guides, videos, and more information to begin to teach the different types of stacks involved in WSSA competition (https://www .speedstacks.com/instructors). Have an activity where you teach the basic stacks and encourage participants to try it out.

- *Relay racing.* Divide participants in teams where they have to hurry across a room, make a stack, then come back to their team. The first team whose members all make a stack first wins.

- *Sorting.* Encourage participants to sort the cups by color or pattern. This can be incorporated with another activity at the end during cleanup. By sorting and organizing the cups, you can reinforce math skills such as counting and putting the cups in different columns or patterns. ("Replacement Cups," n.d.)

TRANSITIONS

Why Are Transitions Important?

A transition can mean several things. Typically, in youth development it refers to moving from one activity to another. That could mean a middle schooler moving from one class to another, or a toddler asked to stop playing with blocks to come to lunch. A transition can mean a change of environment, such as a new room, new school, or new living space. Transitions can also refer to new expectations such as the new rules, legal and otherwise, that arise from becoming an adult. Transitions are hard for everyone. People like their habits and routines. Transitions often mean moving from something we really like, reading a book or watching TV, into something we don't care for as much, like going to work.

In an article with the nonprofit Child Mind Institute Dr. Michael Rosenthal, a neuropsychologist, said, "For kids with autism the world is just an incredibly confusing and overwhelming place, so the need for sameness and predictability is adaptive." With changes in a routine, they may react strongly with tantrums, tears, and outbursts. Dr. Rosenthal calls this "cognitive inflexibility." Individuals with autism have the ability to hyperfocus—they often have strong interests and can do the same thing for hours at a time. This is both an advantage and a disadvantage. The ability to focus is wonderful for productivity, but the world does not often provide that amount of solitude and hours for work. Dr. Rosenthal also finds that transitions are hard for those with sensory processing challenges, like autism or attention-deficit hyperactivity disorder (ADHD). If a student is easily stimulated, the changes with a transition can seem sudden and fast. They may act out because they do not feel in control of their environment and are overwhelmed (Martinell, 2019).

Transitioning to Adulthood

Lavinia Gripentrog is the transitional specialist for special education for the Utah State Board of Education. Before this position, she spent eleven years in a post–high school position teaching students with moderate to severe disabilities. "Most of the time it's a pretty small population of students that go onto post–high school. . . . Most students will graduate with a diploma, and that includes students on the spectrum. If they earn a high school diploma then they are not eligible for services any longer," Gripentrog said. "Only students with severe cognitive disabilities qualify for the alternate diploma and quality for post-high school services" (conversation with author, May 2019).

In post–high school the students with Gripentrog had work-based learning experiences. Sometimes that was volunteering or paid or unpaid internships. Other times it was just being in the community. Students would learn independent learning skills through real-life opportunities. Gripentrog listed some post–high school skills they taught like:

- Self-advocacy (e.g., "What do you do when you need help?")
- Grocery shopping (e.g., buying their own lunch)
- Transportation (e.g., riding the bus)
- Technology on a phone (e.g., text to speech and speech to text, teaching students to text)
- Finding a job (e.g., interviewing)
- Navigating the Internet (e.g., performing a search online)

This type of education could be provided by a library. Librarians can connect individuals to transportation services or resources on careers. Programs can be offered on how to find a job, interviewing, and creating a résumé. Librarians are experts on finding information, and there are many program opportunities of teaching on how to determine between real and fake news, finding a job, researching schools, and much more. Libraries are full of books on topics such as cooking, cleaning, household maintenance, budgeting, and all those many skills vital to live independently. Libraries could host these post–high school classes and be a community center where these young adults can practice what they learned in school.

Library Program and Service Ideas for Encouraging Transition Skills

Libraries can encourage transitions and make those transitions easier with both environmental and programming adaptations. The goal should not be to remove all obstacles for any issues someone with autism may have transitioning; that's not only impossible, but it does not help them learn.

Some environmental adaptations for transitioning follow:

- *Greeting area.* Set up a table or area that can help patrons walking into a program room transition into that program. That could be a sign greeting them, a rug on the floor, a table with handouts near the door, music in the background of the program room, or a shift in lighting. These environmental

PHOTO 2.2. Visual clock.

changes can train the patron's brain that, "I'm entering this new room where there will be a library program. This is where I need to go and what I should expect."

- *Picture schedule.* Create a picture schedule to put in the room that uses symbols to show what will happen during the program. Consider physically removing those symbols as each activity is completed. This picture schedule could also be in places like the circulation desk, which describes the steps for using a self-checkout system. Or there could be a visual reminder of rules in the library, such as a hand over the lips to remember to be quiet, or an X over feet to say "No running."

- *Visual clocks.* Set up a clock, not a digital timer, but a clock with minute and hour hands. There are specialty visual clocks like the Time Timer (see Photo 2.2), which uses color to show on the clock how much time has passed.

Some programming adaptations for transitioning follow:

- *Songs.* Have an opening song, closing song, and/or song for transitions. When I would run programs for older children and teens, I would use Laurie Berkner's "We Are the Dinosaurs." That song had an opening with big, bold stomping sounds, like dinosaurs pounding on the ground. That song was a sign to the group that they needed to walk (or stomp) to the next activity.

- *Provide extra time for transitions.* Give a few minutes for the program participants to adapt to something new. Announce the change and then give them a minute to process the information. Do not rush the change. When people arrive at your program, give them some additional time to see and move around the room. This extra transitional time can let them know that a library program is starting soon.

- *Reminders.* When closing a program, remind the participants that they are returning into the library area. It may be confusing when the participants can be noisier or run around in a program room but not the general library. Remind them that there are different rules for the program room versus the rest of the library. If your library does programs in the same space as other activities, create some kind of environmental change like a banner, sign, or other type of tables or chairs to designate this transition from library to program.

SOCIAL SKILLS

When Anna Decker Smyth, an adult with autism, was asked what her biggest struggle with having autism was, she talked about how her diagnosis affected her socially (conversation with author, July 2019).

My biggest struggle having autism is feeling deeply isolated from others. I don't know how to nurture relationships the way neurotypicals do and so those whom I classify as my closest friends generally categorize me as a casual friend and sometimes even just a distant acquaintance. I've spent so much of my life feeling lonely because of this incongruity, and it has actually caused me a lot of relationship problems (especially pre-diagnosis) with siblings, significant others, coworkers and employees thinking me aloof and even arrogant or malicious, which couldn't be further from the truth. I have the softest, kindest heart and want nothing more than to have a strong social network and support system. I just fail miserably at knowing how to create and maintain one.

Autism can be isolating. As described in Chapter 1, the word *autism* came from the Greek word "autos" or "self." Individuals on the autism spectrum struggle with verbal communication (Alli, 2019). They may not pick up on idioms, sarcasm, or nonliteral ways of talking. This means they may not get the joke or may be the butt of the joke. Those with autism have a high likelihood of having other comorbid conditions, like anxiety or depression, which can further that feeling of being separate and alone. Those with autism spectrum disorder (ASD) also have brains that may take in more input from the world. A social situation with chatter, movements, underlying meanings not clearly spoken, and unspoken expectations on social niceties can make a party seem like a gauntlet to walk through and try to survive.

Libraries can be a place to combat that loneliness and build up social skills. "Because we often struggle with social situations, we need help building and maintaining that sense of community," Smyth said. "Libraries have an incredible opportunity as public gathering places to facilitate conversations, events and more that empower autists" (conversation with author, July 2019).

Social Clubs

One way to facilitate those conversations is by having a social club. These can be a variety of different subjects and models, and more specifics on types of social clubs will be covered in later chapters. These clubs do not have to be complicated. Do not overthink and plan. Focus on the larger goal of the club: a means to encourage social skills and help people make new friends.

A social club at the library can lead to activities outside the library. Eric Stoker, an adult with autism, described what he would want in a library program as "an autism social group." In that group Eric said that "they can talk about what they want to do . . . and make friends and stuff. Maybe they can say 'ok guys' want to go bowling after we read a book?" (conversation with author, May 2019).

A social club does not just have to be for individuals with ASD. By inviting others, awareness and empathy can be spread to those outside the autism community. Anna Smyth recommends for libraries to "host a group conversation led by autists where we can learn about each other. Invite neurotypicals to participate in these events and activities with us" (conversation with author, July 2019). In this situation, those with autism guide the conversation, while librarians take a hosting and facilitator role.

Encouraging Social Skills by Observation

I ran an anime club for eight years as a youth services librarian. Every other week I'd have local teens come by after school for the club. It was often so boisterous I'd have to close the door shortly after we started because the noise would go through the library! The teens in anime club were very social and formed close friendships. It was a club with activities but also a social club. I did not create the teen anime club specifically for individuals with disabilities, but they were always welcome.

Years after starting the club I got a call from a mother wanting to bring her son with autism to the club. She was looking for ways for her son to interact with peers his age, and he was an anime fan. I warned her about how the club was noisy and sometimes the teens could be very energetic, but also encouraged her to bring her son. The first time he came he was very nervous; his mother left him at the door and went to another part of the library to read. I introduced him to the other club members, who were very polite, and after introductions the biweekly activity started. I noticed he remained quiet, and while he sat at tables with others, it was at the far end by himself. I conversed to him some and he was included, but he didn't say more than a few words the whole activity. He would come to the club alone and leave alone.

I was concerned that he felt left out or uncomfortable, and after that program I expected I wouldn't see him again. But then two weeks later he was back. Like before, he didn't participate much, and during part of the program he sat in the corner and read manga. Once again, I thought this would be the last time I saw him, but at the next club he was back. He was quiet again, would say hello and then retreat. After this program I sought out his mother. I told her my concerns.

"Is your son enjoying anime club? Is he doing OK with the noise?"

She chuckled to herself and said, "Oh he's doing great!" I was puzzled.

"But he doesn't really talk to anyone, just sits in the back."

I thought she may have reacted negatively with this information, but she smiled.

"That's great! He's participating."

This teen came back for a few more clubs with similar behavior, quiet, just observed or sat in the room. Eventually, he had a conflict with the date of the clubs and he stopped coming. As I learned more about autism later, his behavior and his mom's words made more sense. He *was* participating. He *was* doing well. He *was* learning social skills.

For this teen, observing and being around teens his age, even if he wasn't speaking, was being social. He would watch his peers and through that could pick up mannerisms, jokes, and new words. Watching an anime with members or doing some art at the table made him feel part of the group. Speaking wasn't necessary. He was in a safe space doing things he enjoyed with other people who also enjoyed them. He was "doing great."

That experience helped me reframe how we learn social skills. Most of our learning of social skills is not through formal lessons, but by listening and observations. Infants learn how to speak not by speaking, but by watching others speak. Those learning a new language pick it up quicker by immersing themselves in that language. And we can encourage social skills with autism not by forced talking, role plays, or classes, but by having them be in safe spaces around their interests and peers.

SAMPLE PROGRAM IDEA THAT INCORPORATES SOCIAL SKILLS: NEXT CHAPTER BOOK CLUB

Libraries and other organizations across the world are already hosting Next Chapter Book Clubs (NCBC). These are community-based book club programs targeting teens and adults with intellectual disabilities. Created in 2002 out of Ohio, Next Chapter Book Clubs expanded beyond that state and into other countries. For more information see https://www.nextchapterbookclub.org.

Materials:

To start the club: Internet and phone
To run the club: Books and a space to meet

Instructions:

1. Contact Next Chapter Book Clubs to become an affiliate. Afterward, NCBC will contact you over the phone to talk about plans. A licensing agreement must be signed before moving forward. Affiliates must abide by the NCBC standards.

2. Determine what library staff will be involved in the book club. Each club needs two facilitators. Make sure the staff who are facilitating

can work this program around their schedule and be committed for the long term.

3. Facilitators must complete a required online training to participate.
4. After facilitators take the training, there is a follow-up 30-minute phone consultation with NCBC staff.
5. Market your new Next Chapter Book Club both in the library and outside of it. Make sure to connect to nonprofits and other organizations out in the community like your state Developmental Disabilities Council.
6. Have your first club meeting. (Next Chapter Book Club, 2019)

Eric Stoker has participated in Next Chapter Book Clubs run out of a local public library. He described how they would read out loud. "They come each week to read . . . right now we're reading Charlotte's Web. It's pretty easy for people with disabilities to understand" (conversation with author, May 2019). NCBCs encourage social skills, interactions, and literacy. Although NCBCs are specifically structured and modeled for individuals with disabilities, any library book club can provide much of the same benefits.

There is a wide variety of different ways to provide library services and programs to those with autism. But when creating those programs, consider aligning them with the goals of caregivers and professionals already working with autists. By focusing on teamwork, transitions, and social skills, libraries can provide community-based learning that can support the individual as they transition and navigate the larger world.

Individuals with autism have unique needs and challenges, just like other patrons who walk through a library door. Each person in the library community is unique, and understanding the person you're serving is the most important part of creating and adapting library programming. You don't need to reinvent the wheel with new programs and services at your library. Use the topics of transitions, teamwork, and social skills as a guide. Use what you already have.

"We're always looking at special programs, but what's already out in the community? If they're really into gaming, or they're really into birds . . . try to find what's available in the community," Gripentrog said. "Recognize that they may need support to access that instead of creating a special something" (conversation with author, May 2019). Learn more about creating and adapting library programs for those with autism in Chapters 4 and 5.

REFERENCES

Alli, Renee A. n.d. "What Does the Word 'Autism' Mean?" WebMD. Accessed February 3, 2019. https://www.webmd.com/brain/autism/what-does-autism-mean#1.
"Become an Affiliate." n.d. Next Chapter Book Club. Accessed September 1, 2019. https://www.nextchapterbookclub.org/become-an-affiliate.

Martinell, Katherine. 2019, August 23. "Why Do Kids Have Trouble with Transitions?" Child Mind Institute. https://childmind.org/article/why-do-kids-have-trouble-with-transitions.

"Replacement Cups." n.d. Speed Stacks. Accessed August 30, 2019. https://www.speedstacks.com/store/retail/speed-stacks-replacement-cups.

White, Erin Richard, Barbara Hoffmann, Hannah Hoch, and Bridget A. Taylor. 2011. "Teaching Teamwork to Adolescents with Autism: The Cooperative Use of Activity Schedules." *Behavior Analysis in Practice* 4, no. 1: 27–35. https://doi.org/10.1007/bf03391772.

3

Serving Our Patrons with Autism

I remember the very first time I had a sensory program at my library. It was a sensory story time, targeted at younger individuals with autism and other sensory processing concerns. I spent months researching, planning, promoting, and preparing. I got to the program room early to make sure everything was set up and perfect, then nervously waited.

Happily, the program went well, and the caregivers and children were pleased and ready to come back again. Then the participants exit the closed off program room into the library. I was in the program room cleaning up, not hearing what was outside of the room. After cleanup I walked into the children's area of the library and was approached by one of the parents who attended the program with her three children. She was upset. With a downcast look she explained to me that she was told by a staff member at the customer service desk to "control your child" in response to their noise and behavior. Although she had felt welcomed just half an hour before, now she was questioning returning to the library.

I felt horrible. I talked to the customer service staff member who explained the behavior of the child was against the policy, and she talked to the mother. She was matter of fact and explained she was simply following the rules. Although this staff member's tone may not have been appropriate or sensitive, she was correct that the behavior was in violation of policy. And the mother was also correct in expecting an inclusive space for her child at the library and feeling upset at how she was spoken to. Both sides were right in their own way. I was the one in the wrong. I had spent all those months preparing myself and my program, but not the rest of the library staff. I had informed but not educated them on what I was doing. They did not understand and were simply following the rules.

To be a truly inclusive space people must be welcomed beyond the program room into the whole library. And all staff members must be involved in the process.

Libraries are spaces for everyone. They are one of the few places in society where people of all ages, races, sexualities, and abilities converge in just one area. It's a unique role as a librarian, balancing the needs and rights of the individual with the structure and policies of the institution.

This chapter discusses strategies to make some of the basic librarian tasks more inclusive. It also covers more of the unique needs and brains of those on the autism spectrum. Full inclusivity is impossible—there are too many needs to balance. Despite that, it should be a goal. No librarian is perfect, and mistakes will be made toward that goal. I know I made mistakes.

AUTISM AND COMMUNICATION

Language and communication struggles are one of the earliest signs of autism. Young children do not use gestures like pointing out things like other children their age. They struggle with eye contact as infants. There are also delays in speech and limited vocabulary. Sometimes the speech is monotone, or children demonstrate echolalia, repeating words and phrases others say or things they hear on TV or in a movie.

Researchers from Boston University theorize that the regions in the brain that have to do with hearing do not properly communicate with the areas of the brain that control oral motor activity. They, along with other practitioners, recommend moving, drumming, making sounds, or some kind of activity when trying to speak words. This type of movement is a staple of library story times everywhere, which can be adapted into a sensory story time. These types of activities can encourage oral motor activity and improve the connection between the hearing and oral motor activity areas of the brain (Berdik et al., 2014).

Although more studies are needed, research suggests that those with autism have an enlarged brain volume. Neuroimaging shows that individuals on the spectrum use their right temporal lobe more than their left, which may influence social language behaviors. Whatever the exact cause, those with autism use their brains differently, and this affects how they communicate (Mody and Belliveau, 2012).

Libraries must work to set aside their preexisting assumptions when communicating with an individual on the spectrum. What might seem obvious or simple to someone who is neurotypical can be a challenging feat to someone with autism. Communication goes way beyond words and phrases; consider tone, gestures, cadence, facial expression, and more. To most people, talking is natural. You don't think about it; you just do it. To someone with autism they may have to think about every single thing and concentrate closely on understanding what someone else is saying. It's like being a traveler in a foreign country with different customs and language. Imagine having to do this intensive task continuously, every day; it's exhausting.

In the book *Social Skills and Autistic Spectrum Disorders,* authors Lynn Plimley and Maggie Bowen describe this difficulty and the assumptions neuro-typicals make. "As we form relationships with families, friends and others, there is a number of things we take for granted. We learn to detect mood and appreciate that using a particular tone of voice has an implied meaning. For individuals with ASD, this can be a complicated process" (Plimley and Bowen, 2007).

The authors describe how a sentence can be dramatically different depending on the emphasis of just one word. For example:

I can't find that book.
> The emphasis on the word "I" implies that the individual can't find the book, but perhaps the library staff member can.

I *can't* find that book.
> By more forcefully speaking the word "can't" in this sentence, there is an implication that finding the book is impossible.

I can't find *that* book.
> In this example, emphasizing the word "that" suggests that particular book cannot be found, but they can find another book. (Plimley and Bowen, 2007)

Many adults with autism are nonverbal or have only a very limited vocabulary, which makes the already difficult task of communicating even more daunting. Add in a noisy library where it's hard to hear, comorbidities with anxiety or other health concerns and other sensory distractions, and an individual with autism might not even bother to communicate at a library.

Literal Thinking

Idioms are words and phrases distinct to certain dialects, cultures, communities, or class. The words used in an idiom have meaning that is unclear for outsiders of the communities they are derived from. Idioms are like slang that they're used in particular contexts, but an idiom is different in that it's meaning can't be easily derived. Idioms are also used in both written and spoken language, while slang is primarily spoken. They can vary across generations and culture.

Some examples of idioms are:

- "Over the moon"
- "Light at the end of the tunnel"
- "When pigs fly"

Both idioms and slang are difficult for individuals on the autism spectrum. Plimley and Bowen write in their book, "Phrases such as these can be confusing to individuals with ASD who take things very literally. Any conversation with an individual with ASD will need to be specific and unambiguous" (Plimley and Bowen, 2007).

Other terms that can be confusing to someone with autism is jargon. Jargon are the specific words and abbreviations used in particular fields. For example, in aviation instead of saying the word "lavatory," which refers to the bathroom on the aircraft, they say "lav." For an outsider, the word "lav" has no meaning. Libraries are full of jargon. Here's just a sample of what might be said in a public library:

- RA (Reader's Advisory)
- Catalog (referring to an online database)
- Circ Desk (circulation or information desk)
- Cart (book cart)

What other jargon can you think of?

We use jargon because the entire word takes longer to say. It cuts down on time to condense two words into one word, or even just two letters. There is nothing inherently bad about jargon, but using them does not give the patron the best customer service. They may result in the patron having to ask for clarification, or even worse, not asking questions and getting lost or confused. These words have little meaning to a person without autism and are particularly challenging to someone whose brain tends to interpret things literally.

Unfortunately, trying to be very polite in our interactions with patrons can still cause confusion. We speak ambiguously to be polite. We ask questions when we should make direct statements. We use hedge words like "suppose," "probably," "partially," and "sometimes." Consider this interaction using ambiguous and polite terms.

Library staff member: "How are you doing today?"
Literal-minded person: "My stomach hurts and I'm feeling tired from yesterday."
Library staff member: "Oh I'm sorry."
Literal-minded person: "Why are you apologizing? It's not your fault."
Library staff member: *Feels flustered and unsure what to say.*

The library staff member in this interaction said nothing wrong. They were engaging in polite speak, small talk. But they were also ambiguous. They were saying hello by asking "How are you doing today?" They apologized to the statement "My stomach hurts" to express empathy. These are the social niceties that we are taught from a young age to say. When someone else does not follow the prescribed script in these interactions, it can cause confusion and frustration. It's like someone on stage who is following their lines, talking to another actor who refuses to say the words on the script.

Plimley and Bowen write, "We often use polite language implying that there is a choice when actually there is not." Think of when you're talking to friends about where to go out for lunch. "Should we get Italian?" you may ask. You really want Italian, but you phrase it as a question to be polite. A library example would be asking "Can I show you where the book is?" when you really mean, "I'm going to walk over to the book, please follow me" (Plimley and Bowen, 2007).

We don't think about using slang, idioms, jargon, or polite language; we just say it. These phrases are interwoven in our everyday discourse. It takes conscious effort to be more direct and specific when speaking. Mistakes will be made, but that's how you learn. If you end up saying something that causes confusion and frustration, simply apologize and try again. Understand that if someone corrects your language they are not attacking you personally.

Internal Communication

Communication in libraries is both external, like to the public, on the library website, or at an outreach, and internal. Internal communication is between colleagues, supervisors, and employees and can occur at a desk, e-mail, staff meeting, and more. Inclusivity is both outward and inward facing.

J (2019), an autistic library associate, gives this advice for libraries:

Remember that people of all neurotypes differ in their learning and communication styles. At my library, our staff meetings are mostly verbal. Occasionally, visual aids will be used, but it's not common. Librarians will describe something physical instead of just showing it to us. This is extremely hard for many autistic people to understand.

So, if you have a basket of signup sheets and prizes for a summer reading program, bring the basket into the meeting and show us what's included. If you're trying to get us to understand a new software feature, bring a laptop in and show us. Walk us through processes. Use props.

Allow enough time for people to write down notes and process what you're saying. Don't just ramble through the entire month's upcoming events and expect us to memorize every program and when it's happening and how it works. If you do meeting minutes, send out the minutes.

And be timely. Don't give us information two weeks after we needed it. When patrons ask us questions and we don't know the answer because you haven't told us yet or you just rattled it off in the meeting yesterday and didn't put it in writing anywhere . . . we are going to be very flustered.

Clear and inclusive language helps more than those with autism, but all staff. To summarize J's advice some simple changes in internal communication include:

- Use visual aids in meetings like props, slide shows, and handouts.
- Walk through processes step by step.
- Allow time for staff to ask questions.
- Have a printed agenda available for reference and note taking.
- Send out an agenda in advance. After the meeting, send out the meeting minutes.
- Put things in writing. Consider written instructions of processes at the customer service and/or reference desk.

REFERENCE INTERVIEWS

The reference interview is a vital role of library staff and an opportunity to help the public. A positive or negative reference interview can impact the perception of not only that librarian, but libraries in general. If a patron gets frustrated in their reference interview or can't find what they need, they may hesitate to ask librarians for help in the future. This section goes over tips to make the reference interview more inclusive. Those tips are quotes from Eric Stoker (2019), an adult with autism.

"Take them on a tour and stuff and explain it."

Getting up and out of your seat behind the desk if possible. For those who have autism, they may not be able to understand your communication. They may not know what a "BCD" area is or understand the library jargon. Explaining "it's next to the printer" may mean little to someone who is unfamiliar with the layout of your location.

Walk them around, tell them specifically where items are, and physically hand them or point to the exact thing they need.

"Talk slowly and explain it in a simple way."

In a busy library branch, the impulse to speak and move quickly is there. But for those who struggle with understanding communication, they may need extra time. Explain what you're doing when you're searching for their term. Give them the reasons that the item is in a certain area because that is where those types of materials are stored. Explain why you are asking additional questions to their query so you can make sure you understand them.

"Explain the movies and stuff and the CDs. Explain the rules."

Libraries have unwritten rules when housing their collections. Movies may be placed a certain way on the shelf. They also may be divided by age, genre, or rating. One library may sort their Sci Fi and Fantasy titles separately, others may combine them, and still others may not have genres at all. These rules are not clear to the public; they are unwritten. For literal-minded thinkers, having different rules in different library locations is confusing. Like Stoker said, "Explain the rules."

"Have a chart thing that explains where everything is. A map."

For individuals with autism that struggle with communication, a visual map can be very helpful. The map can be color coded based on each genre. This map could be available at various desks or posted on a wall. Along with a map Stoker suggests, "Have an acronym sheet for people with autism." This could be placed with the map and describe better the call numbers and codes used to sort materials.

These tips go beyond helping someone with autism. All patrons can benefit from more clear and direct communication and understanding the rules of how things are sorted.

Here is a sample reference interview between a librarian and an individual on the autism spectrum, with explanations.

Librarian: "What can I help you with today?
This question is more specific and implies that the librarian is there to help.

Adult with autism: "I want a book on World War II."

Librarian: "Are you looking for a fiction book? Like a made-up story set during that time period. Or are you looking for nonfiction, a factual book?"
The librarian explains the jargon in a simple way.

Adult with autism: "I want a story during World War II."

Librarian: "Would you like that story to have lots of pictures?"
Some individuals with autism may have intellectual disabilities, and a picture book or graphic novel may be easier to read. This question lets the adult with autism clarify what they like to read, rather than make assumptions on reading levels.

Adult with autism: "No. I just want to read a story."

Librarian: "I will show you where you can find a few books that you may like."
At this point the librarian can show the patron their screen with some suggestions of books or get up and take them to the location of books on this topic.

After showing the patron the book, Librarian: "Can I help you find anything else today?"
This question allows the patron with autism to ask clarifying questions and lets them know that the librarian can continue to help them.

BEHAVIORAL CONCERNS

Librarians must consider the unique needs of individuals with disabilities, with the rest of the public who walk through the doors. This is difficult when the needs of some affect the needs of others. For example, people on the autism spectrum react strongly to loud noises, but young children in the library or activities in a program can get loud. The actions of one person can influence the actions of another. It is simpler to resolve this tension between needs if one person is deliberately provoking or ignoring the rules of the library. However, for the most part people are simply using the library in a way that's comfortable to them, not causing mischief.

Balancing the tension of a public space with the needs of many is difficult but important. This tension is not only external but internal. Library staff as well as patrons need to feel included. Autistic library staff member J describes the struggle of speaking up for accommodations and changes. More details about J's experiences working in a library will be covered in Chapter 7.

> Very often, when autistic people try to communicate that something is too loud or too bright, we are dismissed as being "too sensitive" and sometimes even told "maybe this environment just isn't right for you" and shown the door. As a result of unnecessarily dramatic and simultaneously dismissive experiences like this, we tend to avoid mentioning anything like this. We "power through" and end up burning ourselves out. My shifts are only 4 hours long, but at the end of them, I am usually near shutdown mode.

If both patrons and employees are bringing issues to the attention of library supervisors, they should be listened to and respected. Policies and clear communication channels can help with respecting and including anyone who is within the doors of a library.

Crafting Library Policy

How do librarians create policy and guidelines that are inclusive to both patrons and staff on the spectrum? First off, they should include those they are making policies for. Is the input from staff being received and considered? Do patrons and staff know where to communicate questions and complaints to? Are there venues for those communications to be anonymous?

Consider these tips to include the voices of diverse patrons and staff in creating policy:

- Allow communication on policy to be received in different formats. An individual on the spectrum may be more comfortable expressing their input in a written format rather than verbally.
- Create specific and clear questions on any forms for feedback.

- Don't ask for feedback for policy if you do not intend to make changes. If you ask staff and patrons what they think, and nothing changes, they may see their input as a waste of time and/or disrespectful. Announce the changes that are made publicly when the new policy is finalized.
- Utilize software to allow for anonymous feedback. One app is called Blind, available on iOS that has an anonymous chat function. Suggestion Ox is an anonymous online suggestion box. Of course, you can also use an old-fashioned suggestion box as well.

Anonymous feedback can be controversial. Some criticisms are that it does not allow for follow-up. A manager who receives anonymous feedback cannot ask for clarification. Anonymity can also allow for unpopular ideas to be exposed that can inspire a different way of thinking (Snow, 2018). In addition, anonymity is important for HR issues, such as ADA noncompliance. If someone with autism feels unsafe speaking up, like in J's experience, having an anonymous outlet for feedback is valuable.

Secondly, reevaluate older library policies. I can speak to this personally when I began a sensory story time. I was told by my supervisor that I was violating the story time guidelines, which specified a limit to the amount of set up and take down time. This guideline was over five years in the past, and based on traditional, preschool story times. I was frequently taking additional time to set up my sensory story time because I was taking extra time adjusting the room to make it more accommodating and putting up picture schedules. I felt frustrated and angry being disciplined based on a guideline that was outdated and did not accommodate different types of programs. I felt the many hours of hard work were unappreciated. Eventually, this guideline was updated, and I ended up providing my input on ways to make it more inclusive.

Finally, when policy is changed, communicate that regularly with staff. Cover it in staff meetings. Make sure the policy is printed, featured on the website, and posted in certain areas of the library. There's no reason to have a policy if no one knows it, or it's not enforced.

Sexual Abuse and Assault

Libraries have a responsibility to protect those patrons who come through their doors. This is a difficult task with struggles in communication, differing abilities, and multiple ages sharing the same space. Of particular concern to those with different abilities and cognition is sexual abuse and assault. As discussed in Chapter 1, puberty affects those with intellectual disabilities equally. Individuals with autism respond to the hormonal changes of adolescence like everyone else, and those hormonal changes can increase sexual desire. This may cause them to act out through indecent exposure or sexual assault. Although the motivations of these actions are unintentional, the effects have real harm.

In the book *When Young People with Intellectual Disabilities and Autism Hit Puberty: A Parents' Q&A Guide to Health, Sexuality and Relationships*, authors Freddy and Sarah Brown write, "While reliable data is hard to come by, all the research indicates that disabled people are more vulnerable to being sexual abused. And a parallel fact (though uncomfortable) is that disabled people are most likely to be the perpetrators of sexual assaults on other disabled people" (Brown and Brown, 2016).

Young people with severe disabilities are vulnerable to sexual assault because of

- Poor verbal and nonverbal communication
- Lack of sex education
- Dependence on support for intimate care
- Having different caregivers across different environments
- Not being believed or listened to
- Being unaware that they can say no

Their lack of awareness and understanding also contribute them to be perpetrators of assault. There is a cyclical relationship between victim and perpetrator. It is not a black and white situation. Libraries must make decisions in this gray area to protect the greatest amount of people. Addressing sexual assault, however, is not gray. It must be immediately addressed, even if the act was unintentional. Librarians must understand that they must protect the vulnerable, while also protecting those with greater capacity.

MAKING THE LIBRARY ENVIRONMENT MORE INCLUSIVE

Inclusivity is not just policy and communication, it's physical layout. There are strategies and solutions to make the building and structure of the library more welcoming to those with autism.

"When you make a reasonable accommodation, you're not just improving the situation for the disabled person. You're improving the situation for *everyone*," said J, an autistic library associate. "It may be life-changing for the autistic person, and only a little nicer for the neurotypicals, but either way, it's an improvement. Nobody is going to say, 'Ugh, it's so calm in here! I can actually hear you talking to me, how terrible! I miss the lights glaring in my eyes so that I can't even see the computer screen!'"

Noise

"The library that is a tomb-like sanctuary of stillness and silence is a relic from the last century," said autistic library staff member J. Although some libraries may be quieter, like those in academia, public and school libraries are typically boisterous and full of sound.

Noise is a sensory issue, and what is quiet to someone who is neurotypical may be overwhelming for someone with autism. Their brains do not process external stimulation the same way. There are many noises in a library. Noise can be the hum of the computers and lights, patrons talking, books moving, library programming, the clicking of typing, the squeaks of library carts, and much more. Combined all together, these sounds can be a large distraction.

"Modern libraries are community hubs, which is good, but can become harmful if not done thoughtfully," said J. "In my library, we have dedicated meeting rooms and study lounges (for groups), but all the other areas are pretty busy. The only space that is a 'quiet zone' is the adult collection, where the computers are also located. This is on the second floor. The circulation area, where I work, is located in the ground-floor lobby, where the noise level exceeds safe levels more often than not."

J pointed out one solution for noise—having dedicated quiet zones. Adults wanting to work or students studying will also benefit from these quiet zones. They can be walled off with glass or furniture away from the children's areas. Signage specifying the quiet areas should be used.

There are other potential solutions to noise:

- *Educate the patrons on noise.* J said, "I wish we had a big, colorful sign at the entrance, reminding children to use inside voices and 'walking feet.' Instead, they come crashing through, running and screaming and knocking things over, as if it's a playground. I'm not one of those grumpy, stuffy curmudgeons shushing everyone, but I do think children are no longer being taught how to behave in public spaces. Adults can be just as loud, of course (though they don't make that high-pitched shriek that toddlers do)." Teens can also benefit from this education. Consider having a back to school orientation for teens that frequent the library after school.

- *Provide noise-deafening items for individuals who request it.* Noise-canceling headphones and ear plugs can help library staff sensitive to noise who must work out near the public. Of course, individuals working directly with the public cannot wear them. However, if a reference or circulation desk has an area facing away from the public, the staff may benefit from such items.

- *Determine an agreed-upon noise level.* Noise levels are subjective. What is too loud for one is fine for another. Compromises must be made. Talk as a staff how loud is too loud. At what point do library staff intervene? Other questions to consider are:
  - Are there certain times of the day where there can be more noise? Less noise?
  - What noises are acceptable from children? From teens? At what levels of noise from young people will the library tolerate?
  - What noise level is accepted from staff? Are library staff talking too loudly?

Dedicated Spaces

Libraries have numerous dedicated spaces: adult nonfiction, children's area, public computers, maker spaces, program rooms, circulation areas, and much more. Are any of those dedicated spaces available for those who may need a sensory break? In addition to quiet zones for the public, libraries should consider dedicated quiet spaces for staff. This goes beyond anyone with autism, but all library staff need a break from the public. Does library staff have a room where they can have quiet? If a library does have this type of room, it's most likely a shared space.

Shared staff spaces can be problematic. Evidence from research out of the Queensland University of Technology's Institute of Health and Biomedical Innovation shows the negative effects of open office plans. Researchers found that that employees with a shared open space have a loss of privacy, lower work productivity, overstimulation, and can even have health issues. The Queensland study found that these symptoms were found in 90 percent of employees. Open floor plans are often used because of lower construction costs. The open floor plan may not change in a library building, but in library staff rooms managers should be aware of the effects of coworking (Oomen et al., 2008).

Shared spaces can become more private if there are dividers between computers, or cubicle walls. Library staff should also be encouraged to respect the privacy of others and to keep their voices down when they are working back there. It should be understood by all staff that if someone has headphones in at their desk, they are not to be interrupted unless the request is particularly urgent.

Lighting

"In my library there is a lowered ceiling just over the circulation desk with several pot lights that shine very brightly and very hotly," J said. "There have been numerous complaints from staff and patrons alike. For neurotypicals, it may just be unpleasant, while for someone with sensory processing sensitivity, such as an autistic person, it can be a hellish condition to work under."

Those without sensory sensitivities may not notice the glare or heat of a light. But they can be very problematic to some. Examine the lighting in your library. Are there blinds on windows? Dimmer switches to change the brightness of lights? Are the lights hot or cool? Do lamps have shades on them?

Consider using lower wattage bulbs, LED bulbs, and utilizing dimmer switches to make the lighting less penetrating and distracting to individuals with sensory issues. Some lighting can be automated so librarians can set a schedule to adjust the lighting without having to physically change it themselves. These changes can benefit patrons and staff. "These are easy fixes," J said. "It doesn't have to be so dramatic or extreme. It doesn't have to be 'if you don't like it, leave,' especially if the autistic person is doing a good job. Such simple accommodations!"

Furniture

Furniture can help make shared and public spaces more private. Instead of large shared tables for patrons to sit at, consider cubbies and nooks. Utilize single chairs, not love seats or couches. Space those chairs with end tables to provide additional distance. Also, choose furniture that is quieter. A metal or plastic desk and chairs may make screeching noises.

As libraries plan for renovations or building new spaces include those with sensory concerns in the planning process.

"I would *loooooove* if the owners of public spaces, businesses, etc. let us walk through their spaces and then asked what we thought," said J. "From harsh lighting to the lack of a quiet decompression nook, we could easily tell you exactly what needs to be done to make your space more accessible."

When changing environments and policies for persons on the spectrum, think about the accommodations they make every day. J, an autistic library worker, said, "Consider how many accommodations—sacrifices, even—an autistic person makes throughout their day. When I ask for the smallest thing, neurotypicals act like I'm being outrageous. Some will even say, 'Why don't *you* make some accommodations too? Why don't you meet us halfway?'" Many people who are not on the spectrum cannot truly empathize with what "halfway" looks like.

J goes on to say in response to others asking her for more accommodations, "This boils my blood faster than almost anything. These people have obviously never bothered putting themselves in our shoes for even a *moment.* . . . If they did, they'd see how much we give of ourselves, how far beyond our limits we push ourselves, how much personal hell we go through, every single day, to make *them* comfortable. The world is already built for them, and yet we're supposed to 'accommodate' them?"

Making inclusive spaces isn't just following regulations and checking off boxes. It's a gesture to those in different communities of empathy and understanding. It's a way of going beyond talking about diversity and inclusivity, to making action about it.

REFERENCES

Berdik, Chris, Jackie Ricciardi, and Devin Hahn. 2014, October 28. "Unlocking Emily's World: The Brink." Boston University. https://www.bu.edu/articles/2014/autism.

Brown, Freddy J., and Sarah Brown. 2016. *When Young People with Intellectual Disabilities and Autism Hit Puberty: A Parents' Q&A Guide to Health, Sexuality and Relationships.* London: Jessica Kingsley.

J. 2019, August. Discussion with author.

Martinell, Katherine. n.d. "Why Do Kids Have Trouble with Transitions?" Child Mind Institute. Accessed August 23, 2019. https://childmind.org/article/why-do -kids-have-trouble-with-transitions.

Mody, Maria, and John W. Belliveau. 2012. "Speech and Language Impairments in Autism: Insights from Behavior and Neuroimaging." *American Chinese Journal of Medicine and Science* 5, no. 3: 157. https://doi.org/10.7156/v5i3p157.

Oomen, V. G., M. Knowles, and I. Zhao. 2008. "Should Health Service Managers Embrace Open Plan Work Environments? A Review." *Asia Pacific Journal of Health Management* 3, no. 2: 37–43.

Plimley, Lynn, and Maggie Bowen. 2007. *Social Skills and Autistic Spectrum Disorders*. London: Paul Chapman.

Snow, Shane. 2018, January 27. "My Company Is Killing Anonymous Employee Feedback—Here's Why." *Fast Company*. https://www.fastcompany.com/40518499 /my-company-is-killing-anonymous-employee-feedback-heres-why.

Stoker, Eric. 2019, May. Discussion with author.

4

Library Programs and Services for Teens with Autism

Libraries can be a haven and community for teens and young adults with autism. Annalise Rice, a young adult on the spectrum, described her experience with libraries (conversation with author, October 2019).

> *Growing up in a small town, with not many friends, the library was my safe haven. Reading books helped me combat loneliness. I was diagnosed with high-functioning autism when I was 15 years old. I had always known I was different from other people. The only problem was I didn't know why I wasn't connecting with others. Libraries were a place where I could go on adventures and connect with characters in a way I couldn't do in the real world.*

This chapter discusses the challenges of getting teens to the library and making them feel comfortable when they are there. Libraries can be places that trigger sensory sensitivities, or like Annalise said, a place where they feel safe. They can be a place where those with autism spectrum disorder (ASD) may feel overwhelmed, or somewhere that they can find friends and community. Even though there are challenges, by bringing teens and young adults in the library, librarians have an opportunity to create lifelong readers and library users.

STRUGGLES OF TEENS ON THE AUTISM SPECTRUM

Teens with autism have different needs and challenges than adults. There are big differences between a teen's brain and body and an adult's. Teens and adults are vulnerable to different concerns. Teens also have less life experience to rely on when making decisions.

Research from a lab in Vassar College by Dr. Abigail Baird compared brains from adults and adolescents when evaluating various scenarios. The teens took longer to evaluate sometimes-risk scenarios like "jumping off a roof" than the adults. Baird said, "What I think happens is that teens just haven't had enough experience to develop the gut feelings that grown-ups can use to make decisions without thinking." A teen walking into the library may not be familiar with the rules and the processes like an adult. They need that experience, but they also need safe spaces. "The adolescent brain is hungry for experience—it's a biological imperative," said Baird. She goes on to say, "One of my greatest concerns is that many parents are inadvertently harming their children by trying to protect them too much. I'd much rather a kid fall off her bike than crash the car" (Baird, 2005).

A parent with a child with autism may have even more concern, because they lack both the experience and the brains to take those risks. Closer knit communities with more parents and caregivers could provide that safety net for children, which our spread-out societies don't have. Libraries are one of the few public gathering places left for a variety of different ages and abilities.

To be clear, all teens have struggles; teens are in a transitional space with their lives and bodies. However, the brains of individuals on the spectrum have additional risk factors that can increase the likelihood of problems. They may struggle to pick up verbal cues and understand communications. They may have been protected and lack some of the experiences a neuro-typical peer has learned. A community of adults and mentors, like those found at the library or in a school, can help mitigate those risk factors. A committed network can build up protective factors and resiliencies to navigate through the rocky shores of adolescence and young adulthood.

Puberty

Adolescence is like toddlerhood. The brain's activities surge and pulse in spikes, pushing the individual to take risks, explore, and move away from their caregivers. Toddlers and teens are more likely to take risks, in positive and negative ways. Parents often speak with exasperation about their toddlers and teens because of this phase they are in. Both toddlers and teens need adults and caregivers in their lives. For toddlers these caregivers help them not fall and hurt themselves. For teens, adults can help them not only hurt themselves but affect those around them.

During puberty the hypothalamus in the brain stimulates the pituitary gland to release hormones. These hormones are called gonadotropins and spread throughout the body through the bloodstream. They increase the production of estrogen and androgen in girls and boys. These hormones cause secondary sex characteristics such as the growth of breasts, body hair, changes in the voice, widening of the hips in girls, and more secretions of oil and sweat. These changes can be startling to those experiencing them. Their bodies are different; their feelings are different (Brown and Brown, 2016).

Puberty is difficult for all adolescents. It is a time of discovering identity, new emotions, changes in the body, emotional highs and lows, and permanent physical changes. All teens will have challenges with this time in their lives, not just those with autism. And not all those with autism will have the same struggles when going through puberty.

In the book *When Young People with Intellectual Disabilities and Autism Hit Puberty: A Parent's Q&A Guide to Health, Sexuality and Relationships*, Freddy Jackson and Sarah Brown write that "children with intellectual disabilities face additional challenges that stem from their increased difficulties in understanding what is happening and how they are feeling. To help them through this period of their life they are likely to need extra support and patience as they learn the skills they need to express their emerging sexuality and make healthy choices" (Brown and Brown, 2016).

Hormones and social and cultural expectations create new worries about romantic relationships and sexuality. Teens with autism may see their peers dating and feel left out or confused. Librarians with groups of teens may be familiar with pairing up and the sometimes arguments and tension created by dating. I remember as a teen librarian I would sometimes spend my time consoling a broken-hearted teen, calming arguments, and seeing groups of teens come together, break up, and rearrange themselves continually. Those were experiences I was never trained for as a librarian, but I did my best. Freddy Jackson and Sarah Brown's book said,

> The nature of their intellectual difficulties mean they will struggle to understand what is happening to their bodies and to communicate their needs. This can, in turn, lead to a range of inappropriate behaviors that leave them at a risk of criticism, rejection or even abuse. For example, they may not fully understand the importance of privacy and so masturbate in public whenever the urge arises. Or they may want to have a romantic relationship with someone and instead of asking them on a date they tease or grope them. (Brown and Brown, 2016)

Librarians, who are often the arbiters and referees of teen arguments in the library, should be aware of these concerns. Of course, teasing and groping can come from any teen, but a young adult with autism may not understand the problem with this reaction. And certain behaviors, like public sexual exposure, affect others in the library. That behavior cannot be tolerated, even if the behavior was performed with no ill intent or understanding of consequences. In those situations, librarians should immediately intervene and contact the caregiver. This may mean the individual with autism is not allowed to attend library programs, particularly with children involved. It may mean the person with autism cannot be in the library without an adult caregiver. In a scenario where the behavior happens repeatedly even after intervention or work by caregivers, there may be the necessary consequence of not allowing the individual to come back to the library. This is unfortunate, but the safety of all in the library must be privileged over the one.

In their book the Browns write, "Learning socially acceptable ways to express their sexuality and communicate what they want is a critical skill, which they may struggle to learn. Or they may never learn these skills and require permanent support with this aspect of who they are." This permanent support may need a caregiver next to the individual at all times when in public. If a teen or young adult with more severe disabilities is present in the library for periods of time with no caregiver, librarians should contact social services. This could be a sign of neglect. It is not the responsibility of librarians to step into the role of caregiver. Librarians should also not directly intervene in socially inappropriate sexual behaviors or feel they are the ones having to teach these critical life skills (Brown and Brown, 2016).

Bullying

A report to Congress in 2017 from the U.S. Department of Health and Human Services said that 46.3 percent of adolescents with autism spectrum disorder were victims of bullying. This number is substantially higher than neurotypical adolescents. The report recommends that "because social interaction challenges are a defining characteristic of ASD, it is important to understand and address the potential needs of all youth and young adults with ASD" (U.S. Department of Health and Human Services, 2017).

The report also gives statistics that 14.8 percent of teens with ASD are perpetrators (U.S. Department of Health and Human Services, 2017). This is a tricky subject because the definition of bullying requires clear intent to cause mental or physical harm to another. In addition, is responding and fighting back after bullying also considered bullying? This topic was explored in a 2018 journal article published in the *Journal of Autism and Developmental Disorders* titled "Autism Spectrum Disorder and School Bullying: Who Is the Victim? Who Is the Perpetrator?" The article states that those with autism and comorbid conditions such as oppositional defiant disorder struggle with emotional regulation (Hwang et al., 2017). By lacking the ability to regulate their feelings, those with autism may act out or react very strongly negative behaviors.

The journal article concludes that "perpetrating behaviors in children with ASD are more likely to result from other factors, such as behavioral problems" and that they are not bullies because, due to confusion with social functioning, they don't have ill intent.

A teen with autism may have problems with motor control and self-regulation and speak rather directly and literally. This combination may lead the individual with ASD to be perceived as being unkind or rude, particularly if the recipient of the verbal or physical attack did not know the perpetrator was on the autism spectrum. The 2018 study examined adolescents with autism in South Korea and found additional supporting evidence to prior research on the subject that "children with ASD have bullying experiences more frequently, both as victims and/or perpetrators than do community comparison children" (Hwang et al., 2017).

Despite the intent, however, the consequences of bullying in the library are the same. Bullying can cause harm, stress, depression, and long-term consequences. A 2015 study reported increased levels of anxiety in people with ASD who had been victims in the past. Bullying also causes difficulties for librarians who must manage the behavior of the library. Librarians may not know what to do or say and feel anxious when particular individuals are in the library. Even if the actions of those with ASD cannot be considered "bullying," librarians still must intervene. Librarians must walk a fine line between protecting the vulnerable and the victims and treating everyone with respect based on their ability levels (Weiss et al., 2015).

Some suggestions for librarians in dealing with bullying that involve those on the autism spectrum include:

- *Encourage friendships.* A protective factor against being a victim of bullying includes having close and positive friendships. For those with autism, however, this can be a struggle since they sometimes have difficulties establishing and maintaining friendships.

- *Explain the library rules.* In a private space, tell the person with autism the library rules around bullying and your concerns. For individuals on the spectrum who are low functioning and have more severe comorbidities this may not be possible. If the young person with autism cannot intellectually understand the rules and policies of the library, explain them to a caregiver.

- *Be consistent.* For neurotypical teens in the library, they may be frustrated if they feel the rules only apply to them, and not others. Try to be consistent in the way you manage behavior for everyone in the library.

Another suggestion relates to theory of mind. The concepts in theory of mind mean trying to understand another person's knowledge, emotions, and intentions. It's a process children go through in their early years where they begin to understand that others are not like them and may react and think differently. Having a strong theory of mind can help individuals understand how to navigate social situations. Some of these skills take longer to develop for those in autism and may never be at full capacity; it is a lifelong struggle. A theory of mind training may include things like interpreting facial expressions, explaining concepts like sarcasm, and discussing and role-playing scenarios (Liu et al., 2018).

A 2018 study published in *Plos One* stated, "Research revealed that adolescents with ASD have limited insights in social processes; they may not be aware of the consequences of their own behavior and thus may bully, without being aware of it." The study found after teaching groups of adolescents a ten-part theory of mind training that participants who participated in the training sessions self-reported less bullying and caregivers reported that the severity of the remaining bullying went down (Liu et al., 2018).

A few simple activities to encourage theory of mind include:

- *Identify emotions.* If there is a bullying incident where the person with ASD was the instigator, ask that person how the victim may feel. Ask them to identify what the victim might feel. Tell them that it is normal to experience multiple emotions at once.

- *Read books with different perspectives.* If you knew the individuals with autism's favorite books or genres, use an example of a character or plot to demonstrate different reactions or thought processes.

- *Reinforce positive behaviors.* If you see a patron with autism communicating or behaving well and following library rules, let them know. If you only call out the negative and never the positive, it can create frustration and resentment.

SOCIAL PROGRAMS FOR TEENS IN THE LIBRARY

When asked what are the biggest needs for teens on the autism spectrum, autism advocate and mother of an adult with autism Cheryl Smith mentions social programs. She lists: "Social skills training, structured social events where they can meet friends . . . employment skills including soft skills for those who are verbal and high functioning" (conversation with author, May 2019). All these types of programs are activities that most libraries are already doing. The rest of this chapter describes ways to adapt, create, and market these programs for teens with autism.

Social skills are something that neurotypical people take for granted. They more easily pick up the nuances of tone and words and can engage in small talk without as much anxiety. These skills were acquired from infancy by observations and interactions—they were typically not explicitly taught. For those with autism, these "natural" skills must be coaxed and practiced. In special education there are many lessons and practice with communication. In such classes students may role play scenarios, watch videos of communication, and discuss theory of mind concepts. Libraries are safe places where teens with autism can take those school lessons to the real world.

Before embarking on social skills programs, libraries should keep in mind that this can be a stressful experience. Lynn Plimley and Maggie Bowen's book, *Social Skills and Autism Spectrum Disorders,* describes this stress. "In supporting individuals to develop social skills, it is worth considering how this may be experienced by the person concerned. You are attempting to teach the individual an area which they are naturally weak and are likely to have had bad experiences." The book goes on to say that some reactions to this process will include resistance to trying new things, sensitivity to criticism, and high levels of anxiety and fear (Plimley and Bowen, 2007).

Some of these fears may be assuaged if the teen is already a user of the library. If they had never used the library before the program, they may be unfamiliar with the space, staff, noise levels, lighting, and need time to feel more secure. Other ways to make the programs more welcoming are to speak to the caregiver individually before. Ask their caregiver if there are any particular concerns or fears and also things that their teen with autism enjoys. Suggest that the caregiver come to the first library program, or stay near the teen with autism as they adjust to their new space.

Finally, libraries should be patient and generous. Annalise Rice, a young adult on the spectrum, gives this recommendation. "One thing I would like to say to those serving people with autism is be patient. Some autists have slower processing speeds while others are super-fast at processing. It is a spectrum after all. Just be kind to everyone despite difficulties that may occur" (conversation with author, October 2019).

Social Stories

Social stories are simple, short, and personalized narratives to help those with autism exchange information and learn what to do. They can make complicated, new, or fearful requirements and transitions easier. They are written in the first person to be spoken aloud and internalize the message. Those with autism may write their own social stories or use stories written by others. There are several ways that librarians can utilize social stories to better serve those on the autism spectrum.

Describing Library Rules and Policies

Library policies may be confusing and generate questions. How quiet is quiet? Why is there a need for a rule? What happens if the rule is broken? Social stories can help people navigate the rules.

This example of a social story is for explaining the library rule of being quiet.

> *Many people use the library. It is not just a space for me.*
> *When it is noisy in the library it disturbs other people.*
> *I will try to be quiet in the library. I will whisper. I will read quietly.*
> *Being quiet in the library is kind and respectful to others.*

Demonstrate the Process of Checking Out Library Materials

Checking out books can be a complicated, multistep process. Consider creating a social story around checking out materials. This could also be illustrated step by step with photographs or picture symbols. Those pictures could be placed near the checkout station or be stored under the circulation desk for those who need help. A book of social stories and visual instructions can be laminated and kept behind the reference and circulation desk when needed.

Sharing the Agenda of a Library Program or Event

Anxiety can arise when those on the spectrum do not know what to expect in a library program. Explaining the program in a social story can help calm those fears and establish expectations.

This example of a social story describes a library book club program.

There are many things I can do at the library. One thing I like to do is go to book club.

> At book club we read books like _____. I read the book first
> before coming to book club.
> We sit in a circle of chairs at book club. I must stay in my seat. At book club
> the librarian talks first. It is important I am quiet when the librarian talks.
> After the librarian talks, I get to speak. I raise my hand before speaking. If I
> don't want to speak that's OK too.
> Sometimes there are snacks at the book club. I can eat the snacks while
> listening to others.
> Library book club is fun and I look forward to coming back _____.

Peer Support Activities

Peer-mediated intervention (PMI) is the academic term for working to increase social skills in young people with autism spectrum disorder. PMI, also just referred to as "peer support," encourages interaction and modeling by pairing or grouping those with autism with their neurotypical peers. A review of popular PMI programs published in 2016 in *Research in Autism Spectrum Disorders* found that "PMI is a promising approach to address social skills in children with ASD, and this approach can be conducted in meaningful real-world contexts," like libraries (Chang and Locke, 2016).

Most library programs could be thought of as PMI; they are places where age groups of all abilities can come together. Even a person with autism being in a library and watching others can provide a certain degree of social connectedness and learning just by observation. If a library does want to target and encourage more PMI, here are some suggestions:

- Coach neurotypical teen volunteers. Before pairing them with someone with autism instruct them on the needs of those with autism, potential challenges, and how to communicate with them.

- Pair teens with ASD with neurotypical teens in the library to assist with homework after school.
- Look at the strengths of those with autism in your library. Perhaps one is very savvy with computers. They can help their peers can help teach computer skills to others.
- Pair a new attendee to a teen library program with a regular teen library user. This teen who is familiar with the processes and people in the library can be a "buddy" and advise and answer questions for the teen with autism.

Peer support activities create connections and help both the neurodiverse and neurotypical. Rice, a young adult on the spectrum, said, "For a long time I have put on a 'neurotypical mask' so that others would perceive me as 'normal.' I have since learned that being autistic is not something to be ashamed of or upset about. . . . I personally don't feel like people my age understand what it means to have autism. I think a lot of people my age could become more educated and accommodating to those who are different from them" (conversation with author, October 2019).

Self-Advocacy

Transition specialist at the Utah State Board of Education, Lavinia Gripentrog works with teens with autism as they transition out of high school. When asked what the most important skills for these youth were, she replied, "Probably the number one thing is self-determination and self-advocacy. . . . Allowing them to make choices and advocate for themselves." Well-meaning parents and caregivers may have kept a close eye out of concern to protect their children. This can lead their children to have less experience speaking up and advocating, because an adult had always done it before.

This skill is important for all young people, but particularly for those with autism, who, as they reach the age of 21, reach the cliff. These adults will have to work hard to navigate services that are no longer there, advocate for accommodations at work and school, and speak up to others. Gripentrog gives some examples of self-advocacy skills their program teaches like "grocery shopping, buying their own lunch, riding the bus, technology on phones, teaching students to text," and there are many more (conversation with author, April 2019).

Some of those skills are facetiously called "adulting," and some libraries have even offered adulting classes to young adults who are now on their own. A 2018 American Libraries article cites many libraries in states like Alabama, Montana, Arizona, Indiana, and more that are now offering classes marketed as adulting. The audience for this crowd is typically ages 16–25 and cover things such as meal planning, sewing, finding health insurance, car maintenance, and more (Ford, 2018).

Self-advocacy is part of adulting. Adults must make calls, navigate websites and regulations, understand policies, and speak up for themselves. ASAN, the Autistic Self Advocacy Network, has toolkits aimed at those with autism for them to know their rights and advocate for themselves on their website at autismadvocacy.org ("Policy Advocacy Toolkits," n.d.).

Some ways for libraries to encourage self-advocacy in those with autism include:

- Marketing any adulting-type classes to the autism community
- Creating an "Adulting with Autism" series and invite caseworkers, specialists, autists, and caregivers to teach them
- Encouraging self-advocacy by listening to those with autism, inviting them to meetings where decisions are made, and letting them make choices in library programs

GEEK PROGRAMS FOR INDIVIDUALS WITH AUTISM

Geek fandoms are universal touchstones that reach across gender, class, race, and ability. These fandoms also stretch across genres of books, TV, Internet forums, comics, video games, and more. Two people may have been raised very differently, but they most likely both know who Batman is. Having geek-related programs in the library is a way to bring more attendees through the doors, and for those with autism it can be a way to encourage learning and socialization.

Young adult on the spectrum Annalise Rice said, "I think that libraries should have programs that allow autists to come together and talk about nerdy things. Some people with autism have a lot of random information in their heads. I feel that if there were a safe place for people to stim and be themselves it would be beneficial" (conversation with author, October 2019).

Anime

DH, a young autistic adult, shares his experience with anime (conversation with author, November 2019).

I really broke out of my shell at my first anime convention. I lived in rural Alabama at the time, where the closest "city" was an hour away from our county. Everyone in my age range there was obsessed with sports and hunting, and were of no interest to me. So the amount of people I had to share any of my special interests without getting ignored or teased was practically nonexistent for me. Once I heard about a place where there are a bunch of people who cosplay and talk about anime and games for not just a few hours, but for a whole weekend? I don't remember being so excited for a get-together before then. Previously as far as any conversation with games and anime go, I would be asked "Is that a Pokémon?" and receive follow-up questions of "Chinese cartoons," which would get tiresome. At the convention, though, I was able to really express my interest in all the costumes and merch and art being shown without being seen as a weirdo. There were also different panels and discussions going around of theories, inside jokes, memes, etc. that can be expressed without judgment. My typical social anxieties were pretty low as well, which was a bonus for me. I was still nervous and by myself (which was stressful in itself, but I cared too much about the anime to care about how many people there might be) but the trade-off for how inclusive everyone was and respectful to others the staff and con-goers were being, it became something I looked forward to each year.

Anime, which refers to animated work that originated in Japan and the artistic style associated with Japanese animation, is an inclusive art form that can bring people of all abilities together. Many of those with autism, like their neurotypical peers, follow anime. Streaming services like Crunchyroll and Netflix have made this art form available to a larger audience. Libraries can tap into this fandom to reach out to those with autism.

Some ideas for using anime, and its book form manga, to attract those with autism to the library include:

- Offering a teen anime club through the library. If there is already an anime club, librarians can work to reach out more to the autism community to attend.
- Building up your anime and manga collection at the library.
- Offering anime art programs at the library. Librarians can also feature anime art drawn by their patrons. This art can be displayed in the library, on their library website, social media, or sites like DeviantArt.
- Purchasing drawing books that teach drawing in anime style.
- Offering programs that celebrate Japanese culture such as language classes, crafting like amigurumi, games of Go, and more. (Rogers-Whitehead, 2018)

Another appeal of anime to those with autism are the characters and stories. Anime covers multiple genres: romance, fantasy, science fiction, horror, and more. It also features characters of many abilities with weaknesses and strengths. The character that does not fit in often turns out to be the hero.

"For anime in general, I'd say the vast amount of characters and different worlds that can be expressed through anime are the main attraction," said DH. He also went on to say that he enjoyed the characters in shonen anime and manga, which are aimed at teen boys. "The protagonists for shonen anime would usually be the underdogs or the outcasts or the goofballs but were feats of unstoppable force/intellect when things got serious, and were really good at what they did, no matter how insignificant or under-skilled other characters perceived them to be" (conversation with author, November 2019).

Dungeons & Dragons and Tabletop Gaming

Dungeons & Dragons (DnD) is a fantasy tabletop game first published in 1974. In this role-playing game each player creates their own character to play. The characters go on adventures and campaigns coordinated by a Dungeon Master (DM), who is the game's storyteller and who sets rules and maintains the fantasy setting.

DnD has grown exponentially in the 2010s. The last five years have seen double-digit sales growth. Since 2014 and the debut fifth edition of the game, plus references in popular shows like *Stranger Things*, it has found new audiences. In addition, platforms like Twitch, YouTube, and DnD podcasts have brought this game, frequently played in basements, out in the mainstream (Whitten, 2019). More libraries are adding DnD to their programs. The game is inexpensive, reaches a wide audience, and promotes the library's geek collections.

DnD is also inclusive and a way to reach out to the autism community. DH, a young autistic adult, describes his experiences (conversation with author, November 2019).

> *I was first introduced to playing DnD at my first anime convention when I was a teen. They followed the standard rules, which I thought was fun, and I was put into a small group so I wasn't too nervous. I was initially overwhelmed by the base rules and hand-calculated statistics, so it took some getting used to. After that game I was introduced to a friend's "Homebrew" quests where the rules were cherry-picked to make sense for the game/quest/world but were simple enough to where the game was quicker paced. . . . This environment was more of what I would consider the "helpful" side of it. It allowed me to delve into a bit of creativity; while I was role playing as a character (based on myself, though), I was simultaneously interacting with strangers in real life. It was similar to playing RPGs online, just with a cardboard medium, rather than digital.*

The rules of DnD helped DH feel more comfortable in that social environment. But also having some flexibility with the rules encouraged his creativity. DnD is in a physical environment that encourages socialization. But it's socialization with a safety net. The rules and characters discourage unstructured small talk, which may cause anxiety in someone with autism. There is also the digital component, particularly recent with the growth in popularity. Gamers can also find guides or create their own on sites like dndbeyond .com (Maxwell, 2018).

DnD is the most popular tabletop game in the world. But there are others that may be of interest to those with autism that have the same strategy and role-playing elements of DnD. Some examples include:

- Star Wars: Imperial Assault
- Claustrophobia 1643
- Res Arcana
- The City of Kings
- Terra Mystica
- Twilight Imperium

There are other tabletop games that tap into popular books like *Lord of the Rings*: Journeys in Middle-Earth and Mansions of Madness, based on H. P. Lovecraft's titles.

Video game programs at the library can also encourage communication and social skills. They will be addressed in Chapter 8.

MARKETING LIBRARY PROGRAMS FOR TEENS WITH AUTISM

Teens and young adults with ASD may not be coming to your library because the programs aren't interesting, or they are unaware of them. They may also not attend because they may not feel comfortable in the library environment. Thus, a key step in marketing programs to any teens or adults with autism is evaluating your library environment.

DH, a young autistic adult, said, regarding library geek programs, "It is also important to know that the sheer existence of these programs may not be enough to entice everyone, or especially a DnD/anime/gamer fan on the spectrum . . . the environment has to not be overstimulating or overwhelming."

DH gives suggestions to librarians wanting to reach out to the community. He offers suggestions such as:

- Low light
- Low noise levels
- Comfortable seating
- Nonoffensive color-schemed areas
- Private areas

DH goes on to say, "Personally, I don't go to my university's library because there's noise from the halls outside, too bright lighting, and a somewhat awkward assistance layout so I wouldn't feel as comfortable going to a DnD session there as I would at a friend's (or my) house" (conversation with author, November 2019).

Strategies and advice for making your library environment more inclusive is covered in Chapter 3.

Reaching Out to Teens with Autism

Unlike adults with autism, most teens and young adults are not in residential facilities but live with their parents or caregivers. Most of them, up until age 21, are in public school. To target adolescents in library marketing, librarians can employ similar strategies as they would when reaching out to other teens in their community.

When advertising geek programs, librarians should consider marketing to the geek community rather than specifically autism groups. This can mean comic book stores, placing posters near the graphic novel section, and sharing in geek online groups and to game stores. For programs like DnD, much of that community is active on Discord, or sites like dndbeyond.com. The anime community is active on sites like DeviantArt and fanfiction platforms like Fanfiction.net or Archiveofourown.org. Librarians can also reach out to cosplay (costume play) groups who are very well connected to the local geek community (Rogers-Whitehead, 2018).

Other suggestions for librarians to reach teens with autism include:

- Partnering with local school libraries for joint programs or shared advertising.
- Sharing information with your local school district's post–high school or center for autism. Some school districts have one or two schools with dedicated special education centers. Librarians can also consider reaching out to their state school board and administration to find out where those facilities are and who to speak to.
- Encouraging teens who already participate in library programs to bring a friend.
- Noting on advertisements for teen programs that teens of all abilities are welcome to attend.

For more information about marketing programs for individuals with autism, see Chapter 6 about programs for adults with autism. The end of the chapter includes strategies for utilizing social media and e-mail lists.

REFERENCES

Baird, A., Jonathan Fugelsang, and Craig Bennett. 2005. "'What Were You Thinking'? An fMRI Study of Adolescent Decision Making." *Department of Psychological and Brain Sciences.*

Brown, Freddy J., and Sarah Brown. 2016. *When Young People with Intellectual Disabilities and Autism Hit Puberty: A Parents' Q&A Guide to Health, Sexuality and Relationships.* London: Jessica Kingsley.

Chang, Ya-Chih, and Jill Locke. 2016. "A Systematic Review of Peer-Mediated Inter-
    ventions for Children with Autism Spectrum Disorder." *Research in Autism
    Spectrum Disorders* 27: 1–10. https://doi.org/10.1016/j.rasd.2016.03.010.
Ford, Anne. 2018, May 1. "Adulting 101: When Libraries Teach Basic Life Skills."
    American Libraries. https://americanlibrariesmagazine.org/2018/05/01/adulting
    -101-library-programming.
Hwang, Soonjo, Young Shin Kim, Yun-Joo Koh, and Bennett L. Leventhal. 2017.
    "Autism Spectrum Disorder and School Bullying: Who Is the Victim? Who Is the
    Perpetrator?" *Journal of Autism and Developmental Disorders* 48, no. 1: 225–
    38. https://doi.org/10.1007/s10803-017-3285-z.
Liu, Meng-Jung, Le-Yin Ma, Wen-Jiun Chou, Yu-Min Chen, Tai-Ling Liu, Ray C.
    Hsiao, Huei-Fan Hu, and Cheng-Fang Yen. 2018. "Effects of Theory of Mind
    Performance Training on Reducing Bullying Involvement in Children and Ado-
    lescents with High-Functioning Autism Spectrum Disorder." *Plos One* 13, no. 1.
    https://doi.org/10.1371/journal.pone.0191271.
Maxwell, Lucas. 2018, June 19. "5 Reasons to Start a Dungeon and Dragons Club
    in Your Library." *BookRiot*. https://bookriot.com/2018/06/19/start-a-dnd-club.
Plimley, Lynn, and Maggie Bowen. 2007. *Social Skills and Autistic Spectrum Disor-
    ders*. London: Paul Chapman.
"Policy Advocacy Toolkits." n.d. *ASAN: Autistic Self Advocacy Network*. Accessed
    November 21, 2019. https://autisticadvocacy.org/policy/toolkits.
Rogers-Whitehead, Carrie. 2018. *Teen Fandom and Geek Programming: A Practical
    Guide for Librarians*. Lanham, MD: Rowman & Littlefield.
"Social Stories." n.d. ABA Educational Resources. Accessed November 18, 2019.
    https://www.abaresources.com/social-stories.
"Starting High School." n.d. Supporting Autism Spectrum. Accessed November 18,
    2019. http://supportingautismspectrum.weebly.com/uploads/7/3/2/4/7324834
    /starting_high_school.pdf.
U.S. Department of Health and Human Services. 2017, October 1. "Report to Con-
    gress: Young Adults and Transitioning Youth with Autism Spectrum Disorder."
    https://www.hhs.gov/sites/default/files/2017AutismReport.pdf.
Weiss, Jonathan A., M. Catherine Cappadocia, Ami Tint, and Debra Pepler. 2015.
    "Bullying Victimization, Parenting Stress, and Anxiety among Adolescents and
    Young Adults with Autism Spectrum Disorder." *Autism Research* 8, no. 6: 727–
    37. https://doi.org/10.1002/aur.1488.
Whitten, Sarah. 2019, March 16. "Dungeons and Dragons Has Found Something Its
    Early Fans Never Expected: Popularity." *CNBC*. https://www.cnbc.com/2019/03
    /15/dungeons-and-dragons-is-more-popular-than-ever-thanks-to-twitch.html.

5

Workplace Opportunities and Challenges

Overall, the statistics for individuals with disabilities in the workplace are grim. Despite wanting to work, many people find barriers to employment such as availability of jobs, types of employment, lack of accommodations, hiring practices, transportation, and more. The Disability Compendium, a Department of Health and Human Services grant-funded project from the Institute on Disability at the University of New Hampshire compiles disability statistics from federal and other agencies in one place. Their 2018 report summarized the gaps in employment between individuals with disabilities and those without (Lauer and Houtenville, 2019).

The difference in the percentage of employed with and without disabilities that are working ages 18 to 64 years is 40.2 percentage points. That's a big gap. This 2017 statistic published in the Disability Compendium only references individuals with disabilities who live in the community, not in residential care. When looking at the population with disabilities as a whole the divide becomes even bigger (Lauer and Houtenville, 2019).

For adults with disabilities living in the community, only 37 percent are employed. The 37 percent includes any type of employment, full-time and part-time. This number is lower when you break it down for those with cognitive and intellectual disabilities, like autism. Only 27.8 percent of adults with cognitive disabilities were employed as of 2017 in the United States. These statistics are shown in Table 5.1. It's unclear how many of those adults with disabilities have a desire to work, or the ability. However, that statistic shows there is plenty of space for improvement (Lauer and Houtenville, 2019).

The Department of Health and Human Services published another report in 2017 about young adults with autism. They provided more autism-specific statistics around employment. The report stated that "only 58 percent had

TABLE 5.1. Civilians with Cognitive Disabilities Ages 18 to 64 Years Living in the Community for the United States and States, 2017

| State | Total | Employed | | State | Total | Employed | |
		Count	%*			Count	%*
U.S.	8,836,223	2,456,526	27.8	MT	29,667	11,630	39.2
AL	178,431	35,092	19.7	NE	47,616	18,160	38.1
AK	21,349	6,646	31.1	NV	72,846	23,596	32.4
AZ	179,499	48,682	27.1	NH	39,528	14,501	36.7
AR	125,105	26,715	21.4	NJ	183,725	49,747	27.1
CA	841,455	220,446	26.2	NM	74,490	19,349	26.0
CO	137,116	48,231	35.2	NY	458,785	112,637	24.6
CT	87,951	25,160	28.6	NC	291,082	74,360	25.5
DE	23,692	6,444	27.2	ND	15,272	6,522	42.7
DC	17,266	5,461	31.6	OH	381,824	109,574	28.7
FL	544,751	132,938	24.4	OK	139,709	39,449	28.2
GA	272,576	67,869	24.9	OR	135,308	39,337	29.1
HI	24,264	6,588	27.2	PA	408,643	124,066	30.4
ID	60,595	20,354	33.6	RI	38,929	12,840	33.0
IL	279,394	80,953	29.0	SC	152,489	39,157	25.7
IN	210,430	61,599	29.3	SD	20,308	9,075	44.7
IA	76,400	28,289	37.0	TN	232,505	54,788	23.6
KS	80,461	29,581	36.8	TX	649,519	185,543	28.6
KY	188,637	39,506	20.9	UT	67,595	28,095	41.6
LA	152,166	37,053	24.4	VT	22,339	8,690	38.9
ME	59,906	16,333	27.3	VA	207,192	61,524	29.7
MD	144,842	47,251	32.6	WA	218,054	64,899	29.8
MA	192,629	54,270	28.2	WV	81,457	15,040	18.5
MI	330,345	86,579	26.2	WI	154,713	52,853	34.2
MN	146,963	61,501	41.8	WY	18,265	6,722	36.8
MS	111,186	21,363	19.2	PR	149,258	23,129	15.5
MO	206,954	59,468	28.7				

*The percentage of people employed with cognitive disabilities.

Source: U.S. Census Bureau, 2017 American Community Survey, 1-Year Estimates, American FactFinder, Table B18120; https://factfinder.census.gov. Based on a sample and subject to sampling variability. Used with permission.

ever worked during their early 20s compared with those with other types of special health care and service needs, including emotional disturbances, speed and language impairments and learning disabilities (all greater than 90 percent) as well as intellectual disabilities (74 percent)." The early twenties are a prime time for people to be building their career. Young adults with autism were employed at lower rates than other individuals with different types of cognitive and intellectual disabilities (U.S. Department of Health and Human Services, 2017).

In addition to the lack of employment, the DHS report stated that "only 36 percent of youth with ASD had ever participated in postsecondary education or training of any kind between high school and their early 20s." This can be a certificate program, college, or trade school (U.S. Department of Health and Human Services, 2017).

There is a large gap in services and opportunities for individuals with disabilities to find full and meaningful employment. The work to fill that gap involves government, nonprofits, colleges, schools, and libraries. Libraries have an opportunity to work with other agencies to build that bridge between high school and career. This chapter addresses some of the specific barriers to employment and suggests strategies and ways libraries can assist.

HIRING PROCESS

Barriers to full employment for individuals with autism start right at the beginning: the hiring process. Eric Stoker, an adult with autism, worked as a substitute shelver for Salt Lake County for years. He was hired in 2013, but the hiring process was stressful.

His mother Karla Stoker describes Eric's experience.

It was a paper and pencil test when he first took it. But for Eric that paper and pencil test he could never pass. The question said what book is "between" or "after"—which are not concrete concepts for people with autism. He took it several times . . . and then he asked for an accommodation. The library got HR and they gave him an accommodation to shelve the books instead of taking the test. He was able to shelve the books in half the time than it was required to take the test and got everything right.

Those with autism, like Eric, can struggle with mobility and other physical issues, like gripping and holding a pencil and writing. This could be overcome by using a computer to type, or a practical test, like which was provided after Eric asked for accommodations. His mother Karla added that applications "are all online now which is great for Eric since his handwriting is a struggle."

Eric's experience also demonstrates another barrier—communication. Speaking up and asking for accommodations is stressful, but fortunately Eric asked. As addressed in Chapter 3, those with autism are more literal minded, and the vagueness of the hiring questions in the shelving test caused confusion. Some of that confusion was created with words like "next to." Next to on the right? Left? Underneath? The broad terms can be interpreted in multiple ways.

Other strategies for making the library hiring process more inclusive are:

- Providing a quiet place to take the test.
- Making sure the interviewee is aware that accommodations are available at the beginning of the process.

- Offering tests online as well as on paper.
- Conducting the interview at a place that is accessible through public transportation.
- Collaborate with local agencies that work to help individuals with disabilities transition to employment. These agencies can help prepare the individuals for interviews and what to expect during the hiring process.

Another piece of advice for making the hiring process inclusive is offered by Carol Ruddell (2019), the former ASPIRE project director with the Utah State Office of Rehabilitation. She worked closely with the United States Department of Education to promote education and employment for individuals with disabilities. Carol tells employers to be flexible.

Be ready to think outside of what you've always done. Carefully consider the standard job announcement. Requirements such as having a driver's license, lifting 50lbs or typing 50 words a minute, may not truly reflect what is expected in the position. Keep the announcement to what the job really is. A traditional interview can be intimidating for everyone. What are alternatives to questioning someone in a conference room? How about modeling the tasks to be completed and seeing if someone can accompany and do the tasks? Too often interviews only focus on that interview room. Increasing the applicant's comfort may be easily done by providing a tour, making introductions, describing a typical day in the business, etc.

Making an inclusive hiring process is not just good library practice, it's the law. The Americans with Disabilities Act (ADA) prohibits unlawful discrimination at all steps of the process, including the job application, the interviews, questions for candidates, and what the employer sets out as appropriate qualifications for the position. More information about the ADA will be covered in Chapter 8.

TRANSPORTATION

Another barrier to employment for people with autism can be transportation. Some with autism will have no issues passing the tests and driving, but others may struggle. One condition that can be comorbid with autism is epilepsy, which legally restricts someone from getting a driver's license. Autism does not inherently legally prevent a person from driving; however, other comorbid symptoms of autism may make it difficult. A person with autism may struggle with transitions and multitasking. They may be sensitive to certain sounds and light and get particularly frustrated with other drivers, traffic, or changes in their routine. Without a driver's license and reliable transportation, a teen or adult with autism may struggle to find and keep a job.

A 2016 article from the *Transportation Research Record Journal* studied the transportation needs and challenges of adults with autism. They found through interviews and surveys "the vital role of transportation in the lives of persons with ASD, especially as they seek to navigate the often-difficult transition to adulthood" (Coordinating Council on Access and Mobility, 2019).

Some of the transportation issues these surveys found were:

- Absence of transport options
- Lack of understanding and familiarity with public transportation options
- Cost factors
- Safety concerns by parents about their adult children with autism spectrum disorder (ASD)

Both parents and adult children with ASD expressed frustration in these surveys. The parents did not want to be the main transport for their children. And their children did not want to have to continually rely on their parents or other family members.

Transitional specialist Lavinia Gripentrog with the Utah State Board of Education works on these transportation issues in post–high school classes for students ages 18–21 still enrolled in public school. She and the staff helped them navigate transportation, and Lavinia said concerning gaining independence that "a big part of that was learning to ride UTA (Utah Transit Authority) independently."

Some libraries, particularly in urban areas, are near public transportation. But many are not. Transportation is not just an employment issue for someone with a disability but affects education, social lives, and much more. If a library does not see many individuals with disabilities walk through their doors, it may be because they have no way to get there.

Libraries can assist to overcome the transportation barrier by:

- Providing bus schedules and public transportation information
- Assisting individuals to map out routes
- Partnering with local transportation agencies to provide discounts or other incentives

There are federal and local grants and funding in transportation for individuals with mobility concerns. The United States Department of Transportation runs the Coordinating Council on Access and Mobility (https://www.transit.dot.gov/ccam), which is a partnership of federal agencies that works in transportation for people with disabilities and seniors. The Coordinating Council provides grants, training, and resources to local and federal agencies to make accessible transportation.

ENVIRONMENTAL CONCERNS

When Eric Stoker (2019), an adult with autism who has worked at a public library, was asked what he didn't like at the library, his response referred to the environment. He described the little kids "crying" and "squealing." He said when walking into one particular busy branch, "It was just weird. I didn't feel right at home with it."

Librarians may over time become immune to such noise. The cacophony is just the regular background noise to their job. However, this noise and bustle may be a barrier for employment for an individual with autism. They may struggle with concentrating and completing tasks. The work may be draining and stressful.

Here are other environmental concerns for individuals with autism:

- Spacing between bookshelves and desks
- Fluorescent lighting
- Collaborative staff working area with no walls or privacy
- Textures and sounds from walls and floors

It is difficult for librarians to address all these issues. Libraries are public spaces for everyone with noise and movement. However, there are some things that can be done.

Some ideas to provide better environmental accommodations include:

- Use LED lighting instead of fluorescent lighting.
- Have blinds on windows that can adjust the lighting outside.
- Allow opportunities for cubicle walls or some kind of separation in the staff room.
- Have a quiet space in the corner for shared staffing areas.
- Make sure that shelving is spaced with enough room for individuals with mobility issues to safely navigate.
- Allow for noise-canceling headphones in certain library areas.

Employment specialists at government agencies like Vocational Rehabilitation can also provide other suggestions. The IRS also offers up to $15,000 to businesses who wish to make architectural changes to make the space more accommodating. And, of course, ask the individual working at the library what they would suggest making their workspace more peaceful and inviting.

NETWORKING

As the cliched phrase goes, "It's not what you know, it's who you know." Networking and creating relationships is a vital part of finding employment.

Many jobs are never posted but filled through referrals and recommendations. Someone who does not have a big network, but still has the skills, may struggle. Those with autism may particularly have a hard time because they may not be mainstreamed in public school, they are separated from their peers, and their hobbies and interests may differ from others their age.

In addition, those on the autism spectrum may struggle with social skills, so networking and small talk do not come naturally. Small talk and sharing of social niceties are expected in networking. Anna Smyth, an adult with autism, described how small talk in work meetings was particularly stressful, so she would prepare scripts in her head to get ready. She would have some prerehearsed conversation starters, open-ended questions, and other small talk ready to use when the social situation called for it.

"Oftentimes what students and individuals and students lack is social capital," Gripentrog said. "They lack that network. . . . Because they lack that social capital, we need to help build that. That's where I think a library could help that come in. If a library can help with that networking and then an agency can come and do that support piece." That agency can be a school district for students in post–high school or near graduation, a vocational rehabilitation facility, a nonprofit, or others.

Libraries are community hubs where people from all different types of employment come together. They provide a neutral space for free networking. Librarians also know what's happening in the community and could give personalized recommendations of people or places for individuals to connect to.

Lavinia describes this role of a library as a mentor, neutral party, and place for referrals. "For example, if . . . [a library] were connected with other agencies, nonprofits, businesses, talking to them about an individual and asking them 'is that someone you would be interested in?'"

In addition to being that space for networking, libraries can also offer programming around finding a job. Consider a class on public speaking, or a speed-dating-style networking event, or opportunities for mock interviews.

LACK OF APPROPRIATE EMPLOYMENT

The unemployment rate of individuals with autism is not just high because of the barriers in hiring, transportation, or other concerns—but by individual choice. If there are no jobs that interest or excite the individual, they are less likely to try to seek them out or stay with them. Lavinia Gripentrog, who helps high school students with disabilities, finds that her students "get pushed into the three Fs." Those three Fs are food, filth, and flowers. Those Fs stand for positions in fast food, cleaning, or gardening/landscaping.

"We have a tendency with those students to put them in these menial jobs. We don't want to limit our students with disabilities to those three areas." If someone is in a job, they are not happy with, like one of the three Fs, they act out. An individual with autism may become stressed, anxious, and depressed, and then the employer or agency just thinks they have behavior issues, when they would have performed just fine with a better fit for their strengths and interests.

Gripentrog believes that agencies need to focus beyond job skills and those numbers like the employment rate. An organization's numbers of clients they have helped find jobs may look great, but are the numbers more important than how a person feels in the job, or their capacity for growth? "Probably the number one thing is self-determination and self-advocacy," Gripentrog said. "You can teach that to a student no matter what their disability is. Allow them to make choices and advocate for themselves."

Libraries, with their diversity in programming and collections, offer many opportunities for discovery and finding one's strengths. Librarians can get to know their patrons on an individual level and can recommend titles, and even types of employment, that appeal to them as a person, not just a statistic. "In terms of employment I think it's like anything else," Karla Stoker said. "We develop neurotypical employees, understand what they struggle with and what they do well. I think if we're using our gifts then we are successful. So really, for all of us, it's about identifying what those are."

GOVERNMENT RESOURCES

There are government agencies that can be partners with libraries to hire, train, and retain individuals with disabilities. Although libraries have many purposes and serve all populations, some agencies, like Vocational Rehabilitation (Voc Rehab) agencies, have a very focused goal. Libraries need not feel they have to start from scratch but can rely on other's expertise.

"If you plan to target hiring of people with disabilities," Carol Ruddell said, "then seek out the support or training that can be provided by experts. Each Vocational Rehabilitation agency in the country has a business specialist. These are experts in job analysis, accommodations and more. They can also distribute job announcements to be sure it will reach your intended applicant pool. Those same specialists often offer workshops or trainings to provide a broad foundation of information, and then offer customized support for specific situations."

Vocational Rehabilitation (Voc Rehab) agencies also can help recruit and advertise for positions. Although many individuals with disabilities regularly use the library, many may not use their local Voc Rehab agency. They may not know of opportunities, and many positions are not advertised at all. The library can be a connector to these job openings. "If you want to specifically identify an individual who may be a good fit, then again, contact Vocational Rehabilitation or the developmental disability agency in your community," Ruddell said. "They have clients who are job ready and are looking for employment. It they haven't found employment in the traditional job posting methods, they may be perfect for a more selective introduction to the position."

In addition to Voc Rehab, there is federal funding for WIOA, the Workforce Innovation and Opportunity Act (https://www.doleta.gov/wioa). This program is administered by the US Department of Labor through its Employment and Training Administration. It provides funding for vocational rehabilitation services along with populations such as youth or low-income individuals. The goals of WOIA are to work to eliminate barriers to employment through education, economic development, and workforce investment. This can mean providing training to job seekers, assisting employers with hiring and retention, and reimbursing employers for hiring individuals in the program. Libraries may be able to have the salaries or other costs of individuals with disabilities reimbursed.

The U.S. Department of Labor also has an Office of Disability Employment Policy (ODEP), which supports initiatives for employers wanting to hire individuals with disabilities. Their work includes:

- *Employer Assistance and Resource Network on Disability Inclusion (EARN).* Educational service for employers that offers free training on recruiting, hiring, and retaining people with disabilities. It also has job postings libraries could utilize.
- *Job Accommodation Network (JAN).* Another platform that provides advice on workplace accommodations.
- *Workforce Recruitment Program for College Students with Disabilities (WRP).* Connects businesses and federal agencies across the country to find qualified candidates in postsecondary education for positions.

In addition to potential reimbursement through programs like WIOA, libraries may be eligible for tax credits for hiring individuals with disabilities. The Work Opportunity Tax Credit (WOTC) is a federal tax credit available for employers. Some states have specific tax credit programs in addition to the WOTC. Your local Voc Rehab center would be able to provide you more information about potential financial incentives.

"Be creative and work with the resources in your community, like Vocational Rehabilitation, the Developmental Disabilities Councils and agencies," said Ruddell. "Partner to find the best employee for your business, who just happens to have a disability."

Individuals with autism are an untapped resource for employers. Libraries can play a vital role in helping them with developing job skills, connecting them with resources, and providing referrals and recommendations. They can be a hub for federal and local agencies assisting individuals with disabilities in areas of employment. Finally, libraries can go beyond recommendations and references and be an employer.

REFERENCES

Bernick, Michael. 2019, January 15. "Effective Autism (Neurodiversity) Employ-
    ment: A Legal Perspective." *Forbes*. https://www.forbes.com/sites/michaelbernick
    /2019/01/15/effective-autism-neurodiversity-employment-a-legal-perspective
    /#1dd4fa6b76c1.
Lauer, E. A., and A. J. Houtenville. 2019. *Annual Disability Statistics Compendium:
    2018*. Durham, NH: University of New Hampshire, Institute on Disability.
    Accessed August 1, 2019. https://disabilitycompendium.org.
Lubin, Andrea, and Cecilia Feeley. 2016. "Transportation Issues of Adults on the
    Autism Spectrum." *Transportation Research Record: Journal of the Transporta-
    tion Research Board* 2542, no. 1: 1–8. https://doi.org/10.3141/2542-01.
"Policies & Programs Overview." n.d. Coordinating Council on Access and Mobility.
    United States Department of Transportation. Accessed August 18, 2019. https://
    www.transit.dot.gov/ccam/policies-programs.
"Report to Congress: Young Adults and Transitioning Youth with Autism Spectrum
    Disorder." 2017, October 1. U.S. Department of Health and Human Services.
    https://www.hhs.gov/sites/default/files/2017AutismReport.pdf.
Ruddell, Carol. 2019, July. Conversation with author.
Stoker, Karla. 2019, May. Conversation with author.
U.S. Census Bureau, 2017 American Community Survey, 1-Year Estimates, American
    FactFinder, Table B18120. Accessed August 1, 2019. https://factfinder.census.gov.

6

Library Programs for Adults with Autism

There is a great need for services and programs for adults with autism. In the U.S. Department of Health and Human Services report to Congress on transitional services for teens and adults with autism, they listed an "acute need" for services such as:

- Vocational training
- Postsecondary education
- Treatment for comorbid conditions
- Transportation assistance
- Housing
- Wraparound and more community services
- Transition supports and more education to early adolescents and their caregivers (U.S. Department of Health and Human Services, 2017)

Although libraries cannot provide housing or medical treatments, they can help meet some of these needs through programming. When individuals fall off the "cliff" and no longer qualify for federal funding through the IDEA Act, they are often left without services and supports. Public schools provide a continuity of care and services for those up to age 21. Students have an individualized education program (IEP), which brings together the principal, teacher, caseworkers, caregivers, therapists, and others all working together for the student's success. A young person with autism has more supports in a coordinated system of care. A young adult does not have the same level of supports, and those supports are not sitting down at a table communicating with each other.

The 2017 National Autism Indicators report examined a dozen services that teens and young adults with autism spectrum disorder (ASD) commonly use. This list included services like social work, speech-language therapy, transportation, and more. Ninety-seven percent of the individuals with ASD studied in the report had access to those services in high school. However, after high school there was a steep drop in access. The 2017 report noted that 37 percent of adults with ASD in their early twenties were "disconnected," meaning they were not employed or in postsecondary education. Twenty-eight percent of these disconnected young adults received absolutely *no* services or supports. They were disconnected and drifting (Roux et al., 2017).

These drifting young adults may find themselves in a public library. A library may be in walking distance to their house and be a place they are comfortable with. This is an opportunity for librarians to provide even more than programming; they can help offer those community services and supports. They can help connect that person to resources and peers. They can help them through that transitional stage and beyond. Libraries provide programs from infancy to old age and can be there for those who may be disconnected from other supports. This chapter provides ideas and advice of library programs for adults with autism.

PROGRAMS FOR CAREGIVERS

The 2017 report to Congress on transitional needs specifically addressed needs of caregivers. The report reads: "Relief is needed for the adverse challenges faced by families and individuals who face barriers to access, coordinate, and finance what are experienced as 'piecemeal' services on their own, or services that, in many cases, they may not even be aware of" (U.S. Department of Health and Human Services, 2017). These piecemeal services may only provide one aspect of care like transportation or medicine, but do not address all the needs of the person.

More adults with autism are living at home than ever before. A generation ago more adults with autism and other developmental disabilities were placed in large facilities called developmental centers. Then a shift happened with states serving those adults with disabilities through more community-based reserves like agencies that contract with the government. More recently more supports and services are more home based and self-directed. Families bring in a range of different funding sources to pay for housing supports (Autism Speaks, 2019). Although this provides opportunities for more unique and personalized supports, it also makes finding those services complicated. It also means that many adults with autism may be living and disconnected from facilities providing those supports. The caregivers at home may not be aware of library services and need more support.

I saw this personally when running a sensory story time almost a decade ago. Over time the mothers and fathers who brought their children to my library program began to bond. They would chat together when we had activities after the story time. They exchanged e-mails and connected on Facebook. They swapped stories and advice. Through no prompting of my own one of the attendees decided to create a caregiver support group. She brought a flyer to the program one day and shared it with the others. This support group met around lunch time and was aimed at caregivers of children with autism.

I then realized I was not just running a library program for children with autism; I was running a program for adults. For these caregivers, that half hour after the story time when the kids would play and participate in crafts and other sensory activities was their half hour social group. It was a time where they could share resources and stories with others who could empathize with their situation. This time was also one of relaxation where they could sit down for a minute and read a book or look on their phone. The mothers in my sensory program wanted more than that half hour and decided to create a group on their own.

Caregivers, which can include mothers, fathers, siblings, grandparents, social workers, day care providers, and more, also need support. Caregiving can be a hard, thankless job. It can also be isolated. I heard from some of the mothers during those years of running sensory story time that it was a struggle to get out of the house. Sometimes they didn't make it to the program that day despite their best efforts. Sometimes their library visits were one of the only times they could leave the house, and not worry as much about judgment from others. Even a grocery store trip could be a stressful experience, particularly when handling multiple children.

Those children eventually grow up, and the worry of juggling children at the grocery store may fade, but other tensions may emerge. For a caregiver of a teen or adult with autism—particularly if the diagnosis is severe or there are multiple comorbidities—the stress can lead to additional problems. A study published in 2018 in the *Journal of Autism and Developmental Disorders* found that parents, mostly mothers, "experience a profound number of consequences such as high levels of parenting stress." These stresses over long periods of time lead parents to "report an increase of mental health problems such as the risk of developing a depressive disorder" (Grootscholten et al., 2018).

Caregivers of children with ASD that have high-functioning autism with average to above average intelligence still deal with stress. These are people who have higher IQs, are more verbal, and have fewer comorbid conditions. A 2009 study in behavior modification followed the impact of parents of children with high-functioning ASD. They found that these parents had stress, a higher risk of psychological problems, "and poorer mental and physical health . . . compared to families with children without a psychiatric disorder." Their study found that the children with high-functioning autism had fewer behavioral problems, but internalized problems and were more likely to have depression and anxiety, contributing to that caregiving stress

(Rao and Beidel, 2009). Couple that caregiving stress with the potential likelihood that these parents may be somewhere on the autism spectrum. The diagnosis of autism is genetic, so there is a higher chance of a parent with autism who may struggle with their own symptoms, taking care of a child with the same symptoms.

Caregivers need support. What are ways that libraries can provide that support?

Guardianship Support

Many of those with autism will need care their entire lives. When these children turn 18, they may be an adult in the eyes of the law, but developmentally they are not. These young adults need legal guardians to sign documents, make decisions around medical care, and be a legal representative. The process to become a legal guardian can vary from state to state and can be complicated. Libraries, as resource centers, can be a place to help families navigate this process.

Cheryl Smith (2019) and her husband are legal guardians of Carson, their adult son with autism. Cheryl describes her experience becoming a legal guardian and shared a picture (Photo 6.1). "The process used to be very expensive and cumbersome. Families had to get separate attorneys for the parents and the disabled adult and pay expensive fees." Through her work with the Autism Council of Utah they advocated for legislative change in the state. "Now, if the adult is considered severely affected, they do not have to have their own attorney and the fee is only $35. It used to cost families thousands of dollars."

PHOTO 6.1. Cheryl Smith and her family after becoming her son Carson's legal guardians.

There are also other legal options of limited guardianship, where caregivers can only make decisions in certain areas like medical care. Another type is conservatorship, where the caregiver is a conservator and manages the finances of a person with a disability. The conservator only makes financial decisions, not personal decisions like medical, career, or educational choices.

Although Utah families may not have to pay thousands of dollars, families in other states may have to. And they may not know what to do when their child turns 18.

The Autism Council of Utah provides a guide for those with autism transitioning to adulthood and their caregivers (Autism Council of Utah, 2019).

1. When a child turns 18, they must start the Social Security application process. A child's eligibility is no longer determined by the parent's income.

2. Apply for Medicaid.

3. If the young adult is male, they must register with Selective Services.

4. Start the process of guardianship. A first step is getting a letter from a medical provider that explains the diagnosis and needs for help with decision making in vocations, medical decisions, and finances.

The website for the Autism Council of Utah (https://www.autismcouncilof utah.org) also suggests applying for an identification card before 18. This may be a passport, a driver's license, or something else. They will need that ID for those applications and much more.

Another topic guardians and conservators need to consider is a special needs trust. This trust holds assets for an individual with special needs that can supplement their income in addition to Medicaid and Social Security benefits, without affecting their eligibility to receive those benefits. This type of trust can help caregivers set up finances throughout their child's lifetime, even after they are gone (Autism Council of Utah, 2019).

Caregivers are not just providing daily care but must make plans to provide care for many years in the future. This can be anxiety provoking and overwhelming. There are many steps in this process, and families may not know what to do. Libraries can help and provide support for that transition to adulthood by:

• Bringing in experts on the topic from local nonprofits
• Finding a lawyer willing to give pro bono advice to families
• Partnering with local providers such as vocational rehabilitation, schools, and government agencies to distribute information on the topic

Respite Care

Respite care refers to a short-term break for caregivers. It can be formal or informal, such as a break in the home from a friend coming over, or at a special day or residential center. Libraries are not equipped or responsible for providing formal respite care that involves trained providers. However, they can be a place for brief opportunities for a break and can help provide resources for caregivers to find respite care. Like the half hour after my sensory story times where the mothers sat down and chatted, libraries can create the situations where parents and caregivers can take a breath.

Research from the *Journal of Pediatric Nursing* states that respite care can decrease stress among caregivers of children with ASD. However, that respite care does not always have to be formal and structured with trained medical providers. The research said that if caregivers have access to informal care, they may have fewer needs for formal respite care (Whitmore, 2016).

Consider making a separate time or space where caregivers can get a brief respite from their day-to-day work. Here are some suggestions for library staff:

- *Extend your regular sensory programs.* Do not just finish the program when the story time or activity ends, but allow for play and movement in the room. Book the space longer than needed so caregivers can linger.
- *Set out tables and chairs for caregivers.* Consider making a space adjacent to where the activity for those with ASD is occurring. The caregivers can be in the same room but have a space slightly away where they can sit and take a break.
- *Provide unstructured programs.* Having regular unstructured programs like gaming, simple crafts, LEGOs/building, quiet reading spaces, and more can be a way for both library staff and the caregivers to take a step back. Not every library program needs all the activities in a structured schedule. If your library already runs this type of program, make sure those from the special needs communities are aware.
- *Let the caregiver be outside the program room.* For those with ASD who need less supervision or adults, consider relaxing any library policies around having caregivers in the program space or room. Evaluate any existing policies on a case by case basis. Let caregivers sit and read a magazine at a chair outside the room or browse the stacks.

Resources for Caregivers

An important resource for caregivers is access to resources. Libraries are ideal for providing this information; it's part of their mission. Libraries should make sure they have a good selection of up-to-date books to help both individuals with autism and their caregivers. Consider making sure books for caregivers are also included on any autism book displays. Put out brochures of resources near the book displays. More information about collection and resources will be described in Chapter 9.

Here are some recommendations of book titles for caregivers of teens and adults with autism:

- *Adolescents on the Autism Spectrum: A Parent's Guide to the Cognitive, Social, Physical and Transition Needs of Teenagers with Autism Spectrum Disorders* by Chantal Sicile-Kira
- *The Autism Transition Guide: Planning the Journey from School to Adult Life* by Carolyn Thorwarth Bruey and Marty Beth Urban
- *Guiding Your Teenager with Special Needs through the Transition from School to Adult Life: Tools for Parents* by Mary Korpi
- *The Everyday Advocate: Standing Up for Your Child with Autism* by Areva Martin
- *Autism & the Transition to Adulthood: Success beyond the Classroom* by Paul Wehman, Marcia Datlow Smith, and Carol Schall

SOCIAL LIBRARY PROGRAMS FOR ADULTS WITH AUTISM

"Navigating social minefields is probably one of the few things that nearly *every* autistic person struggles with," said J (2019), an autistic adult. "We're all different, but boy that one is a universal hell for us." It is difficult to teach how to fit in. Every social situation has its own unwritten rules. Every social group has its own jokes and history. Gestures, words, stories, jokes—they all have their own meanings that can vary widely with the context, tone or individual. The nuances of groups and communication are things that one has to experience to grasp. Lessons can teach the basics or the outline, but to truly understand what to do or say in a certain situation requires lived experience.

Those on the autism spectrum, like J said, struggle even more with socialization. Those nuances and hidden rules are particularly lost on them. They may make gaffes, be questioned, or even bullied, which lessens their desire to put themselves in future social situations.

Libraries can create opportunities to develop that experience. Like in Chapter 4, discussing social programs for teens with autism, adults can also greatly benefit.

Social Clubs

Eric Stoker (2019), an adult with autism, recommended social clubs in Chapter 2. He described how he wanted libraries to have "an autism social group" where the participants can make friends and continue those friendships outside the library. Along with friends, social clubs provide experience with the subtleties of small talk.

"Eric prepares scripts in his head," Eric's mom Karla (2019) said. "If he's got calls to make the next day, he prepares the day before. He works through those skills." Socializing takes a lot of work and can be exhausting. "Being out in the world and having their mind constantly going," Karla continues, "I don't think they have that time of downtime where they can meditate."

Activities like phone calls, small talk, or any kind of new situation is particularly difficult. There is no script and many pitfalls. Karla says she sees this difficulty when comparing Eric's troubles with small talk and formal presentations. "Eric's done some presentations. He presents no problem, it's flawless. Small talk is another issue." Karla noted that the disability services worker who coordinates those presentations has even remarked not liking taking Eric out to certain avenues to speak. When he speaks there's no problem, so people can think there's no issue.

When creating a social club, consider these two types of social communications: formal and informal, scripted and unscripted. Allow for both types of interactions but understand that communicating off the cuff and informally is a skill that needs additional emphasis.

SAMPLE PROGRAM IDEAS: SOCIAL CLUB FOR ADULTS WITH AUTISM

This is an outline of a flexible and changing program for adults with autism. This club encourages social skills by allowing participants to present on and discuss their favorite topics. The main theme of the program will change from program to program.

Materials:

- Program room with chairs
- Projector and tables
- Name tags
- Supplies related to the theme of the program
- Fidget items (optional)

Instructions:

1. Set up the room in a way that encourages communication. Put the chairs in a circle that face one focal point. Provide name tags for the participants to encourage them to address others directly. Consider putting out fidget items like squishy toys, coloring pages, and markers or others to help individuals self-regulate.
2. Each meeting one member will present for 5–10 minutes on something that interests them. For example, it can be a favorite activity, food, a trip they went on, a movie they saw that they liked, etc.

3. After the presentation everyone has opportunities to ask questions and talk. Consider preparing a list of open-ended questions to help guide the conversation, or fill in the silence if no one has a question.

4. Tie in a short activity related to the presentation. For example, if it's their favorite movie, show short video clips. If it's a food, bring a sample.

5. At the end of the program select one other person to present the next time. Tell them that they will need to decide their topic soon so library staff can prepare something for next time. You can also create a sign-up list and plan several programs ahead.

Neurodiversity Clubs

Neurodiversity refers to the wide variety of neurocognitive functioning in humans. The symbol for neurodiversity is an infinity symbol with a horizontal rainbow, which represents the spectrum and the multitude of ways of thinking. Many college campuses have neurodiversity clubs to support students on the spectrum or those whose brains may work differently. This can include individuals with dyslexia, ADHD, and dyspraxia. Libraries can also host neurodiversity clubs or even partner with local schools and other partners. Some of these clubs celebrate neurodiversity week and advocate for changes in their institutions. They promote self-advocacy and can be a safe space for those that may not fit in (Neurodiversity, 2019).

CRAFTING PROGRAMS FOR ADULTS WITH AUTISM

Knitting

A 2013 international survey of several thousand knitters was published in the *British Journal of Occupational Therapy*. Knitters were asked about their well-being, knitting frequency, and more. This quantitative data was analyzed to find that there was a significant relationship between knitting frequency and feeling calm and happy. In particular, knitting in a group "impacted significantly on perceived happiness, improved social contact and communication with others" (Riley et al., 2013).

Knitting can be a simple way to encourage social activities for those on the spectrum. Since hands are occupied, someone who struggles with eye contact and small talk may feel more at ease. A 2009 study with individuals with eating disorders found that knitting reduced feelings of anxiety and had a calming and therapeutic effect, as well as a sense of accomplishment. Knitting produced a similar effect of mindfulness; it kept the knitter in the present moment. They did not overthink, it kept away negative thoughts, and it allowed the knitter to listen and talk to others without potentially overanalyzing each word (Kingston, 2012).

Many libraries already run knitting programs for teen and adult patrons. Those existing programs can be broadened and made more inclusive or specialized for just those on the spectrum. If the program is broadened, the marketing and outreach will change. Those on the spectrum may not know about the program, or if they can attend. In addition, alternative activities should be provided to expand the existing audience. Libraries should also consider laminating some step-by-step visual instructions on knitting and putting those out on tables. They can also show some YouTube how-to videos on knitting, which may be easier for someone on the spectrum to follow, than verbal instructions. Knitting does not have to be a formal program in a specific room. Knitting supplies can be available for free to borrow at a library reference desk.

If someone does not know how to knit, they can be taught to crochet. Crocheting can create similar projects and uses the same materials, but instead of pointy needles, a hook is used. Some people may find knitting easier, others crochet. Hand knitting with chunky and thick yarns may be easier for beginners. If motor skills are an issue in a sewing group, individuals can help by holding yarn, picking out new projects, or just sitting and enjoying the company.

Papercrafts

Papercrafts include card making, scrapbooking, folding, decorating, cutting, and all the many different types of crafts done with paper. A papercraft program requires less skill than knitting and can be very flexible. A different papercraft can be provided at each program, or libraries can simply provide all the supplies and let the participants make what they want.

Like with knitting, papercrafts provides a social outlet for participants. The pressure of socialization is decreased because the focus is on crafting. Silence is acceptable in a crafting group.

When running a papercraft program, here are some logistical suggestions:

- Put small trash cans out near the tables. Consider investing in some inexpensive trash cans for each participant's area instead of just a few in the room.

- For those who lack motor skills, cutting paper may be difficult. Put out some precut materials. For example, if there is card making, precut the cards beforehand.

- Stamping uses permanent ink. If you are using permanent markers or stamps, put out plastic tablecloths.

- Provide examples of the card crafts. Put samples out for inspiration and guidance.

- Decorations such as stickers, cutouts, ribbons, and other types of extras to add to cards can be expensive. Use coupons or buy in bulk. With larger groups consider limiting the amount of decorations that can be used. With sticker sheets, cut them into small blocks instead of providing the whole sheet.

Giving Back through Crafting

Crafting can go beyond the library to serve the community. By creating something with our own hands and then taking that labor and giving it to someone else, it can connect us with a cause, person, or issue, and provide a sense of pride and purpose.

In the 2009 survey of knitting, researchers found it offered therapeutic potential—but beyond therapy, knitting can give back to the community. Knitters can create warm and colorful items for others, as gifts or for functional purposes (Kingston, 2012).

Knitters can give what they created to numerous groups and organizations such as:

- *Homeless shelters*. In the winter there is a need for warm clothing for the homeless on the street.
- *Hospitals*. Newborns in neonatal units struggle to maintain their body temperature. They are often bundled up or under lights to stay warm. A small knitted hat can help a brand-new baby and be a thoughtful gift that the parents can take home.
- *Knitting for activism*. Knitting has a long history of activism. In 1984 Sojourner Truth taught knitting to refugee camps of emancipated slaves so they could support themselves. Sewing circles during the abolition movement were places where ideas and strategies were planned for political work. This history continues now with hats being knitted for marches such as the March for Science knitting hats in green or blue shades (Segal, 2017).

Papercrafts provide a variety of ways to give back. Consider these options:

- *Holiday cards*. Make holiday cards for senior living centers or to send overseas to veterans.
- *Decorate paper boxes*. Food pantries utilize paper boxes and bags to distribute their food. They may have the option of decorating those boxes, particularly during the holidays.
- *Bookmarks*. Pre-cut out bookmarks and have participants decorate them. These bookmarks can be given out at the library or in library outreach.

Treatment and residential facilities often have volunteer activities with their residents. Consider partnering with a local facility that works with individuals with disabilities. Go out to their facility with supplies or offer to host. By giving back libraries do not only provide opportunities and purpose to patrons, but they can create stronger relationships with community partners.

SAMPLE PROGRAM IDEAS: AUTISM PAPERCRAFT CLUB

This is an outline of a papercraft club that incorporates elements of passive programming. This papercraft club has less setup because there is flexibility on the activities. Regular participants can suggest options of crafts.

Materials:

- Long tables covered in table cloths
- Paper in a variety of colors
- Card stock in a variety of colors
- A set of stamps with stamp pads
- Fine-tipped markers
- Thick-tipped markers
- Crayons
- Colored pencils
- Pencil sharpeners
- Scissors
- Paper cutouts in card stock
- Hand punches in a variety of shapes
- Paper punchers in different sizes
- Stencils, stickers
- Ribbon
- String
- Other supplies as needed

Instructions:

1. Set up the room in a way that encourages communication. Put name tags along the tables if you know who is attending. Distribute the supplies along the table, which may require participants to talk to others to share certain items.
2. Put out examples of different papercrafts that can be made with the supplies.
3. Play music quietly in the background.
4. If there is a specific papercraft that will be made, put out visual instructions and examples of that papercraft. Demonstrate the process beforehand step by step providing both verbal and visual instructions.

MARKETING PROGRAMS FOR ADULTS WITH AUTISM

How do you reach adults with autism? They are not a monolithic group, and all have different interests, abilities, and needs. There is not one market or way to reach them all. However, here are some suggestions to target this audience.

E-Mail Lists/Newsletters

For years I ran a regular e-mail list for the autism community in Utah. It started out as a way to send out reminders for the participants of my program, but then expanded. I subscribed to a number of different mailing lists and would get news, events, and information from local providers, agencies, and educators. Over time the list grew, and other providers learned of it and would send me specific things to share, and people on the list were regularly sending out my information. I would say the biggest advertising and marketing I did with my autism-specific programs were through that e-mail group.

Here are some tips when creating and running an e-mail list:

- *Always use blind copy.* Put your library e-mail in the "To" line and all of the group's names in the "BCC" line. If you do not do that, everyone will be able to see all the e-mails of the group.
- *Don't send too much or too little.* People will unsubscribe if they feel they are getting too many e-mails. Try to aim for sending out an e-mail no more than once a week, or even less.
- *Be careful with attachments and links.* Many spam filters will automatically block an e-mail with a hyperlink in it. They will also block e-mails with attachments, and sometimes the attachments are too large for some in-boxes and will automatically be rejected.
- *Give at least a week reminder for programs.* For big events provide a save the date a month or two in advance, then a reminder a week before. For regular programs that happen on a set date, give a reminder a week before, and if possible, provide the entire year or season's schedule in advance.

Facilities

There are a variety of different housing options and other centers that adults with autism reside or spend time in. More adults with autism than ever are living independently or at home. However, many adults with autism cannot live unassisted and need additional supports.

Some housing models for adults with autism include:

- *Supported living.* This can be a home or apartment where caregivers come and go. This can include a family home or an apartment where the individual with autism lives alone and has regular visits of providers.
- *Semi-independent living.* This type of housing has 24-hour and more intensive supports. Sometimes individuals with disabilities live together in this type of housing or as part of a designated apartment complex.

- *Group home living.* In this model several individuals with disabilities who are unrelated live together with on-site staff who are available at all hours of the day. Sometimes the group home is managed by a provider agency; sometimes parents and other caregivers come together to create a group home.
- *Nursing homes.* Some nursing homes provide housing and support to adults with autism who are older or more medically fragile.
- *Developmental centers.* These large residential facilities are like a college campus and focused on individuals with more severe needs.

There are also providers that provide day treatment and camps to support adults with developmental disabilities. One national provider is Easterseals, and every state has their own providers and nonprofits. NARPAA, the National Association of Residential Providers for Adults with Autism (www .narpaa.org), has information on different residential services and agencies and can help librarians find local centers to contact (NARPAA, 2019).

By advertising directly to these housing facilities and other centers, librarians can target multiple individuals with disabilities at once. There also may be the potential for libraries to go into their facilities and run the program, or the adults with autism to be transported directly to the library.

When I was running sensory programs for teens and young adults, I would sometimes visit a nearby organization that would provide day treatment for young people with severe disabilities. This center had individuals who could not easily travel to other centers or activities. I would go out after school one school year with all my supplies and do a craft or other programs for the participants there. This particular program always struggled with having enough supplies; often they would be broken and not often replaced. The group leaders were always appreciative to have fresh new markers, and a chance for someone else to take the lead with the students. They wanted me there more frequently than I had time—their needs were so great. There are many opportunities for library outreach with the variety of facilities and housing for teens and adults with autism.

Social Media

In addition, or instead of an e-mail list, librarians may want to create a group on social media for their programs. There are many autism-specific groups on Facebook, and it is a place where parents and caregivers interact. In addition to Facebook other social media to consider are Instagram and Meetup. Meetup is an ideal resource for creating specific programs locally.

When creating a Facebook group, think beyond just event reminders and try to make it interactive. Ask the participants their opinions of what programs should be implemented. Poll them. Share interesting articles and promote new books. Respond and interact regularly with participants. Compared to an e-mail list, a group on social media is more a two-way communication channel. It may take more time to operate than e-mail, but it can also make participants feel more connected to the library and provide feedback and ways to improve.

Libraries have an important opportunity to help fill in the gaps of services for adults on the autism spectrum. This is a population that needs more supports and a community that cares. For more ideas on library programs for adults with autism, see the Appendix.

REFERENCES

Autistic Self Advocacy Network. n.d. "Autistic Self Advocacy Network." Accessed November 3, 2019. https://autisticadvocacy.org.

Grootscholten, Inge A. C., Bob Van Wijngaarden, and Cornelis C. Kan. 2018. "High Functioning Autism Spectrum Disorders in Adults: Consequences for Primary Caregivers Compared to Schizophrenia and Depression." *Journal of Autism and Developmental Disorders* 48, no. 6: 1920–31. https://doi.org/10.1007/s10803-017-3445-1.

"Housing and Residential Toolkit." n.d. Autism Speaks. Accessed November 3, 2019. https://www.autismspeaks.org/sites/default/files/2018-08/Housing%20Tool%20Kit.pdf.

J. 2019, August. Conversation with author.

Kingston, R. 2012. "Loose Ends: Unraveling the Benefits of Knitting." *Psychology Postgraduate Affairs Group* 9, no. 85: 18–20.

"Neurodiversity Celebration Week—Pledge." n.d. Neurodiversity. Accessed November 3, 2019. https://www.neurodiversity-celebration-week.com/copy-of-neuro diversity-pledge.

Rao, Patricia A., and Deborah C. Beidel. 2009, December. "The Impact of Children with High-Functioning Autism on Parental Stress, Sibling Adjustment, and Family Functioning." *Behavior Modification* 33, no. 4: 437–51. https://doi.org/10.1177/0145445509336427.

"Report to Congress: Young Adults and Transitioning Youth with Autism Spectrum Disorder." 2017, October 1. U.S. Department of Health and Human Services. https://www.hhs.gov/sites/default/files/2017AutismReport.pdf.

Riley, Jill, Betsan Corkhill, and Clare Morris. 2013. "The Benefits of Knitting for Personal and Social Wellbeing in Adulthood: Findings from an International Survey." *British Journal of Occupational Therapy* 76, no. 2: 50–57. https://doi.org/10.4276/030802213x13603244419077.

Roux, Anne M., Jessica E. Rast, Kristy A. Anderson, and Paul T. Shattuck. 2017. *National Autism Indicators Report: Developmental Disability Services and Outcomes in Adulthood*. Philadelphia: Life Course Outcomes Program, A. J. Drexel Autism Institute, Drexel University.

Segal, Corinne. 2017, April 23. "Stitch by Stitch, a Brief History of Knitting and Activism." Public Broadcasting Service. https://www.pbs.org/newshour/arts/stitch-stitch-history-knitting-activism.

"Services for Adults with Autism." n.d. Easterseals. Accessed November 3, 2019. https://www.easterseals.com/our-programs/autism-services/adults-with-autism.html.

Smith, Cheryl. 2019, May. Conversation with author.

Stoker, Eric. 2019, May. Conversation with author.

Stoker, Karla. 2019, May. Conversation with author.

"Transition to Adulthood." n.d. Autism Council of Utah. Accessed September 29, 2019. https://www.autismcouncilofutah.org/post/transitiontoadulthood.

"Transition to Adulthood." n.d. Autism Speaks. Accessed October 3, 2019. https://www.autismspeaks.org/transition-adulthood.

"The United Voice of the Autism Residential Service Community." n.d. NARPAA. Accessed November 3, 2019. http://www.narpaa.org.

Whitmore, Kim E. 2016. "Respite Care and Stress among Caregivers of Children with Autism Spectrum Disorder: An Integrative Review." *Journal of Pediatric Nursing* 31, no. 6: 630–52. https://doi.org/10.1016/j.pedn.2016.07.009.

7

Beyond Programming:
Volunteering and More

In 2015 I wanted to do more for the autism community than my regular sensory programming. I also wanted to give back to those who had helped me. Over the years of doing that programming I had met many in the community who had given me advice, introductions, and even donated materials. They were passionate about serving those with autism and providing more opportunities for parents and caregivers.

Libraries are natural places for sharing information and resources. Salt Lake County Library, where I was employed, had a large event space perfect for a large gathering. I wanted to gather all these resources in one place, as well as offer a free and fun event to the larger public. In 2015 we offered the first Sensory Faire in partnership with the Autism Council of Utah (ACU) and other community partners. April is the official month for autism awareness, so we made sure the event tied in with those annual festivities. There was a radio DJ, crafts, cosplayers, STEM activities, partner booths, and more. That first year we had over 500 attendees and decided to repeat the Faire in 2016.

In creating the Sensory Faire, I wanted to include those with autism in the process. They should have a say and an active role. Some of the ways we incorporated that community was getting input on what activities to do, someone with autism created a music list, another adult with autism had a booth, and more. In the event we had a story time area outside of the event space, which was quieter. Our storyteller for the event was not a librarian but Eric Stoker. Eric is an adult with autism spectrum disorder (ASD) and was interviewed for this book. His advice and feedback can be found in earlier chapters. Eric picked out his favorite story time books, particularly the Froggy series by Jonathan London and read aloud to the children gathered as seen in Photo 7.1.

PHOTO 7.1. Eric Stoker reading aloud to participants of the Sensory Faire.

Later, when talking to Eric's mom Karla (2019), she told me that whenever Eric gave presentations to the community about what it was like living with a developmental disability, he shared that picture. When I reflect back on the Sensory Faire, I can't tell you what was on the music list, or who all the providers were, or even what crafts we did. But I remember Eric using his "Froggy" voice and reading to the children.

This chapter goes beyond programming, reference, and other basic functions of library customer service. Chapter 7 covers volunteering, employment, and using those with ASD's advice and strengths. It gives practical tips on how to not just invite those with autism to a story time but provide that story time themselves.

VOLUNTEERING

Libraries depend on volunteers for tasks, programs, and much more at the library. Having volunteers benefits not just the library but the person volunteering. Those with autism may be an untapped resource for many libraries. By utilizing their strengths, libraries can better serve their communities and look at their services and structure in a unique way. Here are practical suggestions on utilizing volunteers. This section also describes the experiences of those with autism who have volunteered at libraries.

Volunteer Policies

Libraries should not feel they need to rework their existing volunteer policies for those with autism. But accommodations may be necessary. Some of those accommodations may include a caregiver being present while the person with autism volunteers. Another one is allowing individuals with sensory concerns to wear headphones or earplugs.

Karolyn Campbell (2019), the executive director of the Disabled Rights Action Committee, utilizes volunteers with disabilities in her organization. She describes her experiences using those volunteers.

We know that everybody's needs are different and that this isn't a necessary or helpful accommodation for all folks with autism and can also be helpful for folks with other types of mental or physical disabilities (anxiety, light sensitivity, etc.). We also try to respect that needs and abilities may fluctuate, and we're open to making changes as needed to make spaces more comfortable for a broader range of people. We stock our ADA accessibility kit with earplugs because we've found that these are sometimes helpful for folks who get overstimulated in event spaces.

Like any volunteer a library may have, the volunteer should be matched with their strengths and interests to the tasks to be done. Listen to your potential volunteers on their preferences; do not just assign someone with autism to a certain task because they have that diagnosis. Campbell said, "When I'm working with volunteers, I ask each individual what accommodation they need to have a positive experience working with our organization."

Librarians should make sure their volunteer recruitment process takes into account accessibility. This means recognizing that many disabilities are invisible and assumptions should not be made. Campbell goes on to say, "I don't think that there are many one-size-fits-all solutions. Ultimately, we need to get better at having conversations about accessibility, and we need to be willing to provide accommodations that may seem nontraditional or unconventional."

Lavinia Gripentrog (2019), a transition specialist with the Utah State Board of Education, echoes keeping policies consistent. "A lot of times adults will indulge and tolerate behavior from an individual with autism that they wouldn't tolerate from someone else." Apply a certain standard of behavior to all volunteers. "Find ways to respectfully prompt . . . if they can get away with that in one setting they'll consider that as an adult in a workplace setting. . . . Be consistent and respectful."

Volunteering teaches skills that can be applied to the workplace. It can be an important step to employment. If a library has inconsistent rules and policies, they do not truly prepare their volunteers for the real world. In addition, if other volunteers feel treated unfairly and inconsistently, it can affect the moral of others. Libraries are a place of learning, and volunteering can be an impactful learning experience that goes well beyond its walls.

Library Volunteer Experiences of Those with Autism

A student with autism, who will be referred to as AMO for this section, described his experiences volunteering at the library. "I volunteered at one of the programs and helped out with the little kids. I enjoyed this because I like helping people." Before volunteering, AMO was a library user who found joy there. "I find comfort at the library," he said. "I like that the library offers not just books and computers but programs to experience things. I like when they ask me to help at programs. I like that the librarians don't treat me different than other people who come to the library."

Potential volunteers at the library are most likely already there. Library users may not be aware of the library's volunteer opportunities or not know if the library has need of them. Those with autism may want to volunteer at the library but be uncomfortable asking or performing certain tasks. Libraries should make sure to clearly advertise their volunteer opportunities and let the community know that all abilities are welcome. Those with autism may struggle communicating their needs. They may want to volunteer but have trouble expressing it. Others may not interpret what they are saying correctly.

AMO (2019) describes his experiences with communication. "I don't feel that I am very clear sometimes with what I am trying to say when I talk to people. I don't feel everyone my age understands but I feel like there are some who are trying to understand what I am experiencing." Although librarians may not be able to understand everything someone with autism expresses, it's important they continue to try.

Volunteering Task Ideas

When looking for tasks and projects for volunteers at your library, consider these ideas. They are not specific to those with autism, but some may be of more interest to those with sensory issues.

- Computer assistance
- Running tech events like a gaming program, LAN party, or Minecraft event
- Assisting with homework
- Helping patrons check out e-books and e-audiobooks
- Front-facing out book titles
- Pulling book holds
- Greeting others at programs
- Assisting with story time prep such as cutting out items, going through craft materials, and pulling story time titles
- Program set up and take down
- Refilling any scrap paper and pencil stations
- Decorating for summer reading program or other events
- Sorting returned items on carts so shelvers can return them
- Fixing damaged books or other items
- Cleaning DVDs, CDs, or other discs

- Evaluating library websites for accessibility concerns
- Setting up library book displays
- Helping pick up and maintain the grounds outside the library
- Going through children's craft materials to make sure the glue works, crayons are not just stubs, and the scissors aren't so ruined and sticky that children can't use them
- Shelf read to make sure titles are in the proper place
- Assist in finding missing titles

Some libraries may have restrictions on what volunteers can do. Librarians should also make sure that volunteers are not taking over the duties of regular library staff. Understand and check your library policies before creating new tasks for volunteers.

There are volunteer tasks that go beyond the day to day and the list above. These tasks utilize those with autism in more front-facing roles. They also are ways to make library services more inclusive. Those with autism may see the world differently and can provide a new and fresh perspective that library decision makers need.

Consider these ideas for going beyond tradition library volunteer tasks.

- Copresenting programs with librarians
- Serving on library committees
- Organizing other library volunteers
- Hosting discussions at the library
- Advising on library services to make them more inclusive

Another way to go beyond volunteering and utilizing someone with autism's strengths is to hire them. Details of hiring and recruitment of those with autism are covered in Chapter 5. For more details on what employment looks like from the ground, and from the voice of someone with autism, read ahead.

EMPLOYING THOSE WITH AUTISM

Karla Stoker is not just a mother of an adult with autism, she's a human resource specialist and sees the library as an ideal place for people with autism to learn skills and understand careers. "The library is a great resource, they're right there, they're in our community." There are multiple jobs and tasks in libraries that can appeal to those across the spectrum.

The library also may already be a destination for someone with autism, and perhaps a future career. However, hiring is just the first step of a career. And while the jobs may be appealing to someone with autism, the environment may be too much. Librarians should make sure the workplace is fair, accommodating, and inclusive.

Suggestions for Employing those with Autism

Annalise Rice (2019) is a young adult on the spectrum who works at the Scenic View Academy library in Utah as pictured in Photo 7.2. She finds the library a safe space and enjoys working there. "My favorite duties to do at the library are scan items (I call the scanner my magic wand)," Rice said. She also says she likes to "return books to the shelves and basically anything that lets me do a routine."

Just like other library staff, routines and consistency are important to those with autism. The regular duties provide a sense of calmness and can be helpful for those who struggle with transitions. Librarians should consider making clear the routines with an employee with autism, and not radically changing the routine unless there is clear communication beforehand (Nath, 2013).

In an article published by the Interactive Autism Network, it states that "even after finding a job people on the spectrum may not get the support that they need." Associate professor Dr. Scott Standifer said, "Adults with ASD need concrete instructions about their tasks from their managers." Those concrete instructions should not just be given verbally. Standifer gives the example of Walgreens whose employees have visual instructions. Walgreens also gives their employees options to take short breaks from work. "They're embedding corporate supports and they've building a supportive

PHOTO 7.2. Scenic View Academy's library, the place of employment for Annalise Rice.

and more accommodating workplace and inviting people to join them," Standifer says of the work Walgreen and some other corporate partners are doing (JKP, 2016).

PRIVATE SECTOR PAIRING ADULTS ON THE SPECTRUM WITH JOBS

With unemployment low the last few years in the United States many employers have difficulty filling positions. Those with autism are underemployed and a potential resource for employers. Vocational Rehabilitation and government and nonprofit agencies have done this work for years, but recently some entrepreneurial start-ups have come into the space to help. One, Daivergent, helps connect tech companies with a pool of over 1,000 candidates on the spectrum. That company also helps with skill building, particularly improving social and communication skills.

There are many with autism that want to work but just need the opportunities. Anne Roux with the A. J. Drexel Autism Institute at Drexel University suggests that only 14 percent of those with autism have employment in their community. Libraries are directly in the community and can be that opportunity (Rosen, 2019).

Other suggestions for providing employment supports for those with autism include:

- Remind colleagues of the employee that if the person with autism seems disinterested in talking, or says something "offensive," that is most likely unintentional.
- Speak to the worker with autism one on one if you observe they may be feeling anxious or uncomfortable. Do not call out the discomfort in a group.
- Follow up with conversations with an e-mail to make sure the communication was heard and there's a change to clarify.
- Regularly check in about performance. Just like with other employees, have regular one-on-one chats about performance and expectations of the job.
- When providing feedback, make it direct. Don't imply or allude to potential problems; say it directly, but politely.
- Inquire about sensory distractions. An employee with autism may not feel comfortable expressing their needs and anxieties, so take the first step by asking.
- Write the rules down. Many workplaces have unwritten rules and policies that are assumed that everyone knows. Make sure any rule, policy, and regulation are written down and clear.

Interview with J, an Autistic Library Worker

To really understand the experiences of someone on the spectrum, reading articles, or even this book only gets you so far. Their voices need to be heard. This section contains excerpts of an interview with J (2019), who prefers the title autistic library worker. Her other suggestions and thoughts are also included in other chapters to better describe an autist's experience.

Do you think your employer, coworkers, or patrons view or treat you differently because of your neurotype?

Some do. Since there's such a lack of real understanding out there. . . . Most people, upon finding out, will say, "I would never have known!" That's because I mask my traits at work, and I don't match their expectations. That's one reason I don't hide my status; I want people to walk away from the encounter with a broader understanding of what autism can be.

Then there are the ones who start acting weird around you. They talk down to you, as if your IQ suddenly dropped 70 points in the 5 minutes since they learned you were autistic. They exclude you from activities and conversations. They just generally act awkward, like they're not sure what to say around you.

And worst, they suddenly think you can't do your job. That's the kind of thing that makes most of us not want to disclose at all.

It's very important that people presume competence of the autistics in their life. I've had so many people, professionally and personally, decide not to even give me a chance to do something because they assumed I couldn't or wouldn't want to. They didn't even bother letting me try or asking my feelings on the matter.

The irony is, after a lifetime of this, my wings have been clipped to the point that I actually can't do many things I'm sure I could do if I'd been given the chance. I have not been allowed to grow, learn, and thrive.

This is also the trouble with functioning labels. Every single person who knows me would almost certainly say I am "high-functioning." My mother may be the only exception, and that's because she has seen the struggles I've hidden from the rest of the world.

When I come to work, I am in full mask. You will see me make eye contact, stay on script, force myself not to stim (or if I do, it just looks like "nervous fidgeting" so it's not necessarily a giveaway) . . . and you will think I might seem a bit awkward but you would think I'm managing well enough. I'm "functioning."

Except you don't see me get into my pajamas as soon as I get home because regular clothes are so uncomfortable. You don't see me sit in silent solitude, getting nothing done and pushing away anyone who wants/needs me, for several hours after a hard work shift just to recover from it. You don't see my apartment which is so messy that it would fail inspection without help from my mother. You don't see the laundry she's doing for me because it's just one too many things for me to handle alone. You don't see me making the same tv dinners every night because I can't cook. You don't see me listening to the same songs over and over because it's comforting. You don't see me crying and feeling rejected because, despite staying on script at work, I have literally zero local friends.

Because if the world did see these parts of myself, they would probably decide I'm "low functioning" and stop treating me even a little bit like a human being. I would lose my job, without which I could not survive (disability is not nearly enough to pay my bills). I would lose my apartment and have to live either with my mother (which is extremely unhealthy for us both) or in a group home (which would be hell for me). I would be talked to like a child, not allowed autonomy or dignity. I would not be taken seriously.

When asked about feedback and constructive criticism at work J says:

Many autistic people are actually highly sensitive; we feel deep anguish when we cause others harm; we are so conflict-avoidant that we will agree to things we hate just to please others; we can't handle watching the news or hearing people fight because of the anxiety it gives us.

So in a work environment, we may sense that something is amiss, but we don't know what. If you're displeased with our work, don't expect us to know it if you haven't actually told us. We want to do better; we just need the opportunity. As long as you're not getting emotional about it yourself, we won't take it as a personal attack. We'll welcome the clear communication. It means we don't have to keep wondering!

Employers should understand that while they may feel they are being accommodating, the person with autism may be making even more accommodations. Following a "script," not speaking up, working in areas that are too loud or bright is a heavy mental and physical load. The accommodations work both ways, and managers communicate and give feedback with empathy.

Although there are not as many federal regulations and rules, volunteers need accommodations just like employees. These accommodations do not just benefit those with autism but can create a calmer environment for all staff and volunteers. Everyone needs breaks. Everyone gets overwhelmed some days.

To go beyond diversity to inclusivity there are compromises and accommodations to be made. But instead of looking at accommodations as a barrier, an inconvenience, see those shifts and changes as getting one step closer to all the compromises being made every minute of the day by a person with autism.

REFERENCES

AMO. 2019, November. Conversation with author.
Campbell, Karolyn. 2019, November. Conversation with author.
Gripentrog, Lavinia. 2019, April. Conversation with author.

J. 2019, August. Conversation with author.

JKP. 2016, April 29. "The Importance of Autism Equality in the Workplace—An Interview with Janine Booth." JKP Blog. http://www.jkp.com/jkpblog/2016/04/autism-equality-workplace-interview-janine-booth.

Nath, Sowmya. 2013, April 3. "The Changing Employment Scene for Individuals with Autism Spectrum Disorder (ASD)." Interactive Autism Network. https://iancommunity.org/cs/adults/_employment_and_asd.

Rice, Annalise. 2019, October. Conversation with author.

Rosen, Ellen. 2019, October 24. "Using Technology to Close the Autism Job Gap." *New York Times*. https://www.nytimes.com/2019/10/24/business/autism-jobs-daivergent.html.

Stoker, Karla. 2019, May. Conversation with author.

8

Technology, Autism, and Libraries

Technology has become an integral part of our lives and our libraries. Despite handwriting and fears to the contrary in the early 2000s that it was the "death of libraries," libraries have continued to prosper despite the growth of technology (Staff, 2005). An article in the conversation describes some of the adaptations libraries have made in the digital world. "Libraries digitized their collections and networked their catalogues, exponentially extending the range of materials users could access. . . . They mounted screens to watch movies or to play video games. . . . They wired up their spaces with free WiFi" (Wyatt and Leorke, 2019).

Libraries adapted to the digital world, and they can continue that attitude of adaptation for those patrons who have unique needs. Libraries are places to find both high-tech and low-tech information side by side. They are also a place for the public, where everyone is welcome. That public-facing duty means libraries must be aware of technology trends and make that technology accessible to everyone.

This chapter covers the role of technology in the lives of those with autism. It also discusses ways libraries can be digitally inclusive, and the laws that libraries must follow on that goal. The last part of this chapter covers different ideas to incorporate technology in programs, how to run certain technology programs, and ways to keep those with autism safe on the Internet.

PROS AND CONS OF TECHNOLOGY FOR THOSE WITH AUTISM

Like any tool, technology has both risks and benefits. A hammer is a tool that can be used to construct or to harm. The hammer, like technology, is not inherently good or bad. Having an attitude of reserved openness rather than fear is a positive approach for librarians to take.

For those with autism there have been some startling and sudden changes in treatment and opportunities through technology. Research is still catching up with the long-term potentiality of these new tools. Much of the research is from the education sector, not in libraries. Some research, both qualitative and quantitative, is shared in this chapter, but librarians should keep in mind that there is much that we do not know.

With how much technology is integrated into our daily lives now, it's easy to forget how quickly this all came about. The smartphone is a recent invention; the first iPhone did not appear until 2007. The first iPad not until 2010. Social media is new, too: Facebook debuted in 2004 but did not become mainstream until around 2009. All these tools have affected everyone, not just those with autism. And practitioners, like librarians, are still working to find the best way to integrate them.

From research in education we have learned some benefits from technology in the lives of people with autism.

- *Task management.* Technology can provide reminders, help create schedules, and assist with transitioning from one task to another. This is a benefit to those with autism who may struggle to move from one activity to another.

- *Training.* Those with autism are visual learners, and the wealth of videos on every topic imaginable can be an ideal instructional tool. From a literature review published in the *Journal of Autism and Developmental Disorders* in 2014, it states how videos have been used to teach tasks to adolescents, help teens in school transitions, and train adults in multistep job-related tasks. "Video modeling as an educational tool has been heavily researched over the past two decades," the article states. With more video content than ever before, and available in your pocket, this tool can help those with autism with a wide variety of tasks (Gentry et al., 2014).

- *Location services.* Technology is a tool to help those with autism navigate where to go through maps and GPS services. It can also help them locate caregivers easier than ever before. Caregivers can also keep closer track of those with autism who may be at risk for getting lost.

- *Accessibility settings.* In the classroom and online there are more accessibility settings for those with mobility, vision, or other impairments to learn. This topic is covered more later in this chapter.

- *Calming and relaxation.* Technology, like games, songs, movies, and more, can be used to calm anxiety and help those with autism in social settings. DH (2019), a college student with autism, describes, "I use my phone as a stim device (I would load a game and use it to relax when I have a moment) or I would listen to music to drown out the loud hustle and bustle of crowded areas. I use games as a way of relaxation and as a way to help myself learn skills."

- *Socialization.* Technology can provide a safe space for those on the spectrum to connect with others. Without the potential stresses of small talk or face-to-face conversation, those on the spectrum can find digital communication preferential and less anxiety inducing than traditional forms of communication. Technology can also connect people across long distances and expose people to new cultures and ideas.

There are cons with technology as well. A national U.S. survey published in 2016 found that half of 6- to 17-year-old children with or without autism spectrum disorder (ASD) "used screen media more than two hours per day" (Montes, 2016). Other studies cited in a 2019 behavior sciences study conclude that those with ASD watch more TV and play more video games than their neurotypical youth. Those with ASD are at a higher risk for video game addiction (Stiller et al., 2019).

There are some negative outcomes to screen media use in childhood. The 2019 study cites that screen-based media use "can be linked to a number of negative outcomes in child development, for instance poor academic performance, adiposity, low sleep quality or attention problems" (Stiller et al., 2019). Screen time also has a risk related to issues of online safety, which is covered later in this chapter.

Technology can be used as a tool of inclusivity, but it also can exacerbate learning and outcomes when there is a digital divide. The term *homework gap* refers to diverging outcomes from students who are digitally connected and have families with high digital literacy skills, and those who do not. Two students who started out academically at the same level in kindergarten can take differing paths based on how digitally inclusive they are. A child who grew up with broadband access at home is more likely to have higher grades and be more technologically savvy; they are also more likely to graduate high school (Rogers-Whitehead, 2018). Technology can be a way to bridge inequities, but also exacerbate them. Libraries are an important access point and resource for those who are affected by the digital divide.

AMERICANS WITH DISABILITIES ACT

The Americans with Disabilities Act (ADA) is the civil rights law that prohibits discrimination based on disabilities. It is administered as part of the U.S. Department of Justice's Civil Rights Division. The first ADA law went into effect in 1990 and covers disabilities that include both mental and physical medical conditions (Americans with Disabilities Act, 2019). Those conditions do not have to be chronic or over the course of a lifetime, they just have to limit major life activities.

The ADA has three sections, or titles. Title 2 establishes laws for public entities, which libraries would fall under. As part of this title public facilities have to comply with regulations that cover access to services and programs (Americans with Disabilities Act, 2019). Libraries are held to high ADA standards as public entity with the variety of services they provide. Benjamin Mann (2019), an autistic person who researches disability studies, said,

"Libraries are subject to the broader laws in that area. Accountability is probably very broad given how broad the ADA tends to be." This accountability means that libraries should understand the law and periodically examine their services and facilities to make sure they are following Title 2. There are regulations that are physical and others that are digital. This chapter section covers both types.

ADA Physical Compliance for Libraries

Libraries are most likely complying with ADA laws, such as having handicapped restroom stalls and having wheelchair access to the facility and room between shelves for those with mobility issues. The ADA requires "reasonable accommodations," which can vary depending on the community and location (Americans with Disabilities Act, 2019). There are exceptions for accommodations in certain historical buildings or religious ones. A library must make an effort to have a reasonable accommodation.

Autistic researcher Mann describes the concept of "reasonable accommodations" further. "My understanding is that it's not clearly enumerated . . . some of it comes from particular accommodation requests. People who talk to their doctors and medical professionals and request things like accommodations. Because it's so individualized it's hard to know what accommodations are in that area. The ADA is fairly broad on reasonable accommodations." Thus, libraries may need to respond to requests on accommodations they did not anticipate, or were not clearly spelled out in the law. They may not be able to adjust or adapt to these accommodations, but they must make an attempt.

One part of ADA physical compliance that is not clearly defined are sensory inclusive spaces, which would be reasonable accommodations to some on the autism spectrum. "For those in the autism that's something of a particular concern. A lot of times sensory stimulation is a major concern and you want to have a space," Mann said.

Some examples of spaces that are *not* sensory inclusive are:

- Really bright lights
- Loud sounds
- Multicolored lights
- Fragrances, including perfume and cologne
- Traffic and commotion

Mann said that these can vary a lot depending on the person. He describes his experiences related to sensory stimulation as like a volcano. "The more stimulation it is the higher it rises until it explodes and you can't take it anymore." For more details on creating inclusive spaces see Chapter 3.

LGBTQ+ ACCOMMODATIONS

A 2018 study from the *Journal of Autism and Developmental Disorders* reported that "high rates of gender variance have been reported in autistic people." Among those with autism, women are more likely to have different gender identities than men. The article suggested that individuals born biologically female with autism may feel less comfortable with "feminine" stereotypes and identify more as masculine.

Experiencing gender variance can cause an increase in depression or anxiety. The researchers from the article recommend peer support groups where participants can share their stories. More research is needed in this intersection, but librarians should be aware and not make assumptions or press for specific gender identities (Cooper, 2018).

Benjamin Mann is an autistic PhD candidate whose dissertation researcher studied the intersection of autism and the LGBTQ+ community. His work supports the conclusion from the *Journal of Autism and Developmental Disorders*. "There is a higher correlation of people who are both of those things," and "a lot of those people in that intersection don't feel comfortable with disclosing."

Mann suggests utilizing pronoun stickers in some social situations to provide more inclusivity. This could also be done in e-mails and adjusting habits to not make assumptions on gender. Use words like "they" and "theirs" instead of "she" or "hers."

Inclusivity needs to deal with those intersections of race, class, sexual orientation, gender, and more. Although someone, like Mann, may decide to refer to themselves as an "autistic person," they are more than a diagnosis.

ADA Website Compliance for Libraries

The actual physical space of the library is just one part of their services. Libraries offer a wealth of information, assistance, databases, and more online. For a patron to access their account, place a hold on a book, reserve a room, research a database, and download an e-book, they need to access the library website. If a library website is not accessible, it not only limits their services but it's not ADA compliant.

Just like with physical spaces, the American Disabilities Act has regulations on digital spaces. As more public services come online, this has become an increasingly vital issue, and compliance is scattershot. "One thing that was really surprising to me, I read a couple of months ago that all of the websites of U.S. presidential candidates were not accessible in a way they needed to be. I think that points to the broader need for websites to have increased compliance," said Mann.

How can libraries make their websites ADA compliant?

- *Image descriptions and captions.* An alt tag is for visitors on the website who may have visual impairments, or those viewing it in plain text. Instead of displaying an image, the website shows the alt text which describes the image in words.

- *Basic and plain text versions of websites.* Plain text refers to content that is readable and excludes images and numbers. Using plain text makes websites easier to load and read. Some browsers have options, and there are online tools to view websites in plain text.

- *Basic fonts and colors.* Try to stick with traditional fonts like Times New Roman, Arial, Helvetica, and Garamond.

- *Dictatable text.* This is text that's available for screen readers.

"I know a lot of websites have a problem that those who are blind can't use their dictation software on their websites," said Mann. He also recommends that librarians check out Universal Design Principles. There are ways to embed descriptions in images that can help those who are blind read the screen, plus add more information to those who may be unclear what the images represent.

There are multiple ways to make a website ADA compliant and also ways to test that compliance. Karolyn Campbell (2019) is a PhD student at the University of Utah and the executive director of the Disabled Rights Action Committee. She is going through the process of making sure all of her non-profit's website is accessible.

We're using the UserWay app on our website, and we've added alt text to all of our images. We're currently working with the National Federation of the Blind to test our website on a variety of screen readers. You can learn more about the app at userway.org. I don't think that our website is perfect, but we're trying to think creatively about a broad range of accessibility barriers, and we're looking for ways to improve. The widget is great because it provides so many options—you can use it to read the text (much like a screen reader would), enlarge the text, adjust contrast, adjust text spacing, adjust fonts, pause animations, and more.

ADAPTIVE TECHNOLOGY

"Recent years have seen an increased focus on new developments in information technology, resulting in the emergence of a number of aided devices," states a 2017 article in the journal *Support for Learning*. "The popularity of digital culture along, with the trend towards economic globalization, the advancement of information technology and the development of knowledge-based society has led to the implementation of computer assisted information skills to cope with the challenges in every aspect of life" (Sankardas, 2017).

These supports are adaptive technology. The *Support for Learning* article finds that these devices help young people with autism better communicate in the classroom. These products can also help them reach others at home or in the library.

Assistive technology (AT) is the umbrella term that that encompasses any item, equipment, system, product, or device that helps improve or maintain the capabilities of persons with disabilities. Adaptive technology falls under AT, and sometimes the two terms are conflated. Adaptive technology typically refers to electronic and IT-related systems and are specialty items. An assistive technology could be nontech, like a cane, wheelchair, or ramp.

There are more adaptive tech devices and items than ever before that can be used to make the library and its services more accessible. Autistic researcher Benjamin Mann suggests libraries have "stim toys, fidget spinners, clay . . . a variety of things that people can use for stimming. A lot of times people might not necessarily have stim toys available or might forget to bring them." Stim is short for "stimulation" and can help those with autism self-regulate and cope in an unfamiliar environment. These toys can be left out in a library program, maker area, or can be made available at the reference or circulation desk.

Mann also suggests "looking into the ability to rent things like noise-canceling headphones, or something else that muffles sound." This can be particularly helpful if a library has an open-floor plan without quieter spaces, or a large number of children. If there are items to check out or rent at the library, make sure they are advertised. Someone new to the library may assume they can check out books, but not think a stim toy or a headphone is an option.

Other examples of adaptive tech libraries can use are:

- *Picture Exchange Communication System/Boardmaker.* These two software use pictures to communicate. They are generalized and basic symbols of ideas, verbs, items, emotions, and much more. Those that are nonverbal can point to pictures to share their feelings and requests. Libraries also use these picture symbols to teach specific processes, like checking out a book. The pictures can be printed out and used in signage or programs.

- *Screen-reading and screen-magnifying software.* One well known screen reader is JAWS, and others include OmniPage or ZoomText.

- *Touchpads or trackballs.* These items substitute a standard mouse and allow individuals to navigate the computer with less pressure on hands, arms, and wrists.

- *Adjustable desks and large monitors.* These will allow for better wheelchair access, and a large screen can help those with vision impairments.

There are also accessibility functions incorporated into browsers. For example, Google Chrome has an Image Alt Text viewer that can help librarians find pages that are missing any alt text. Chrome also has the option to enhance webpage colors and offer high contrast. Before purchasing any accessibility equipment, see what is already available through operating software, devices, and browsers. Also, librarians can consider checking out some of this hardware rather than installing them on all computers or devices.

LIBRARY PROGRAMMING WITH TECHNOLOGY

In 2013 I received an LSTA grant from the Utah State Library for mini iPads with my sensory activity group aimed at older children through adults with disabilities. I had read a little research on this topic before writing the grant, and I had ideas of what I wanted to do; but actually, using the iPads taught me much more than any research I did. I remember sitting at a table with a stack of the iPads splayed out, wondering what to do first. Through my experiences I learned that technology can be a helpful tool to encourage teamwork, social skills, and as an incentive. I also learned that technology can never replace a caregiver, teacher, or librarian. Here is a picture of me (Photo 8.1) shortly after I got the iPads and was figuring out what to do!

From my experience here are some practical recommendations for librarians wishing to use tablets for those with disabilities in library programs.

PHOTO 8.1. The author with her mini iPads used in library autism programs.

- *Have a maintenance plan.* Updating twelve iPads at once not only takes multiple electrical outlets, but time. I remember I had just learned about a new app I wanted to try before a library program. I started downloading the app on the tablets while setting up, but quickly realized there would be no way I would have enough time to get the app installed in time. There are mobile device management solutions to update remotely; however, I didn't have those in place. If you are purchasing a larger quantity of devices to use in programs, consider a remote solution to keep them updated and download apps. Other maintenance items to consider are charging. Check to make sure that the devices are all turned off before putting them away after a program, or your next program you may find their batteries are dead. You will also want a charging station with multiple ports instead of having to rely on a few sockets on the wall.

- *Cases.* If a screen breaks on a tablet, it does not only cost you money, it can cause injury. Cheryl Smith, mother of an adult with autism, had an experience where her son Carson cut off the tip of his finger after swiping on a broken tablet. The glass is very sharp. Make sure all your devices have secure cases that can handle being dropped, thrown, or even stepped on. I used Otterboxes on all my mini iPads and never had an issue with them breaking despite many drops.

- *Accessibility functions.* Both Android and Apple have accessibility functions under their settings to make the device easier to read and navigate. For library programming I recommended iOS's Guided Access. This setting locks the tablet to only use one program at a time. This keeps the participants using the app you want them to, and not potentially stumbling on inappropriate content online.

- *Beware freemium apps.* There are many apps that are free to download but require purchases to unlock other content. This can be frustrating to an individual who does not understand why the game won't play or having to deal with pop-ups that interrupt play. Some freemium apps provide more content than others and do not have as many annoying reminders and pop-ups. Investigate apps before downloading them.

- *Use the tablets strategically.* I learned quickly that the iPads could be as much of a distraction as a support in my library programs. I kept the iPads hidden as the participants came into the room and only brought them out if we were using them specifically for an activity, or at the end where there was free play. I would sometimes offer the iPad to an individual as a reward for good behavior, like transitioning peacefully from one activity to another, or helping to clean up.

I found after years of using the iPads in my library programming that they were best as an add-on, an enhancement, rather than the focus of the program. I saw them as a tool, not a requirement for fun and learning. With some programs I would not use them at all. Librarians should look at technology as a way to support the great work they're already doing, a way to make activities more inclusive, and a way to bring the neurodiverse into the library.

Online Safety

Libraries are places with constant Internet access. They serve an important role in helping to bridge the digital divide, and in some communities they are some of the only Internet access available.

This constant access also has downsides—among then online safety concerns. Young people may be exposed to inappropriate content online at the library; sometimes that exposure happens from other patrons at the library. Young people are particularly vulnerable to cyber risks, as well as those with autism. Freddy and Sarah Brown's book, *When Young People with Intellectual Disabilities and Autism Hit Puberty: A Parents' Q&A Guide to Health, Sexuality and Relationships,* addresses this concern. "Due to their more limited understanding, children and people with intellectual disabilities are particularly vulnerable to being taken advantage of over the Internet"(Brown and Brown, 2016). Social cues are already difficult for those with autism to pick up. Online, without tone, gesture, and other nonverbal clues, the messages may be even harder to decipher.

The Browns go on to write, "Social media such as Facebook can be both a positive opportunity for children with intellectual disabilities, and a social and emotional minefield! For children who find socializing anxiety-provoking, the opportunity to connect with others online, and not to have to worry about interpreting body language or how they are coming across is a relief. For others, the rules around privacy and online social etiquette can be difficult to comprehend" (Brown and Brown, 2016).

Digital platforms have their own social etiquette, which can include slang, gifs, memes, and inside joke. Memes and emoji may be interpreted multiple ways. Literal thinkers may struggle in certain online communities and in gaming where jokes, teasing, and one-upmanship are common. This ambiguity can put those who lack as much communication and social experience at risk.

Librarians should consider programs to educate on online safety. There are numerous risky situations online for children and young people with intellectual disabilities, such as online forums, online chats, multiplayer games, webcams, and social media. However, when talking about this subject, librarians should address both the pros and cons of the issue. Speaking with fear and strong negative attitudes toward the Internet dismiss the positives that come from it and may only serve to drive risk behavior underground. "The issue is how to strike a balance between the benefits of going online and the potential risks associated with it," write the Browns (Brown and Brown, 2016).

Some suggestions for keeping individuals with autism safe online include:

- Pairing and seating those with autism next to someone who is neurotypical when navigating the Internet.

- Providing a parenting class aimed at caregivers of those with autism on how to be safe online.
- Recruiting law enforcement such as your local chapter of the Internet Crimes Against Children's Task Force. These task forces are spread out across the United States and can provide free education on digital laws and suggestions on how to stay safe.
- Create a dedicated children's computer area, whose devices are open to all ages. These children's computers have stronger filters than the rest of the computers in the library.
- When roving, pay attention to children on computers who may be at risk.

Video Game Programs

Library programs with video games are a staple at many libraries. I remember doing many of my own teen video game programs over the years. I spent time sorting through the various wires, trying to keep up with the newest PlayStation game, and labeling every single instrument of Rockband because they were easily lost. My concerns during the early 2010s were around wires, game compatibility, and the struggles of setting up the system. Since those years the video game landscape has changed. Less wires, more in-game purchases. Less physical games, more mobile gaming. Video games have changed a lot from my childhood gaming days, but I am cheered that the franchises I loved, Mario and Zelda, remain the same.

The video game market has exploded in the last three years. In 2018 there was a record-breaking 43.4 billion in revenue for the U.S. video game industry, which was an 18 percent growth compared to 2017 (Gera, 2019). Video games have brought new audiences and new opportunities for gamers. In addition to the variety of games, experiences, consoles, and ways to run a video game program, gaming can bring a number of positive benefits to those with autism.

VIRTUAL REALITY PROGRAMS

Virtual reality (VR) is a simulated experience commonly accessed through the use of headsets with a small screen in front of the eyes. Improvements of technology have brought down the cost of these headsets for use in more individual homes and libraries. Research cited in the *British Journal of Educational Technology* describes VR as a "platform for naturalistic social skills training" and finds "effectiveness and features of VR game tasks and settings in social skills training" for children who have high-functioning autism (Ke and Moon, 2018).

VR can immerse the user in a realistic setting where they can practice social skills in a safe place. This immersion can also place the user in scenarios where they are unfamiliar and allow them to have experiences they would not have otherwise. A report from Stanford researchers cites Professor Jeremy Bailenson saying "experiences are what define us as humans, so it's not surprising that an intense experience in VR is more impactful than imagining something." The Stanford study researched people who went through a VR experience called "Becoming Homeless" to see how empathy levels were impacted. Participants virtually experienced the daily trials of those who live on the street. The researchers found that those who went through the experience had more "enduring positive attitudes" toward the homeless than those who read narratives or interacted in a two-dimensional environment (Stanford News, 2018). For librarians interested in this topic the company Floreo creates specific lessons for those with autism and has been used in school settings and therapy.

An article published in 2018 in the *British Journal of Educational Technology* cites a study done with an online single-player game, called Zoo U, "for social skills learning by children with behavioral and emotional problems." The game had various scenes that encouraged social problem solving. The article reports that "the study found a significant and positive effect of the game-based learning problem in enhancing the participants' parent and self-reported social skills, functioning and self-confidence" (Fe and Moon, 2018). In addition to social skills, video gaming can encourage collaborative work and motor skills.

Librarians should consider expanding any additional video game programs to those with autism, or with the collaboration and advice of library users with autism, create one of their own. When creating a library program around video games that is inclusive to those with autism, here are some suggestions:

- Provide headphones or some kind of noise-canceling earplugs. The noises from video games may upset some with sensory difficulties.

- In addition to video games, put out some nondigital activities such as card or tabletop games, chess, and books to read.

- Consider creating a sign-up sheet or bracket for certain games. For example, when playing a game like Super Smash Brothers that is one on one make it a tournament-style play. Having a sign-up sheet can encourage transitions from one player to another.

- If possible, instead of purchasing the games, borrow them. Active attendees can loan out games. There are some games that remain popular for a longer period of time. But many do not, and the video game industry moves quickly with new releases and updates to existing games.

- Buy your own equipment such as the game console and controllers. You do not want to risk borrowing someone else's equipment that you may damage.
- Invite caregivers to these programs, and make a space for them. Set aside a quieter area not only for those with sensory issues, but for caregivers to take a break. This area can include soft chairs, books, magazines, and more.
- Put out a large, visible clock or timer. To encourage transitions, make the time visible so players and watchers know how much time they have left.
- Although wireless controllers can be easier to use, they can get lost more easily. Consider using wired controllers.
- Label library property so it does not get mixed in with any items that are borrowed or brought to the program.
- Avoid long games with puzzles and quests that are designed for single players. Although some attendees may be content with watching another attendee play, some may be frustrated without game play of their own.
- Use projectors. Some TVs are more difficult to use to set up games. Projectors have gone down in price and can be quick to set up. Projectors also allow for a larger screen that increases visibility.

Many librarians are already including video game programs in their libraries. With some adaptations and a different marketing strategy, they can open them up to those with autism in their communities.

When using technology in the library, think beyond compliance and rules. Autistic researcher Benjamin Mann said, "As you might know, there's different models of disability and a lot of the times that disability issues come into libraries go through a medical model." Mann encourages librarians to "see that disability is a product of society rather than the problem being the individual." This "is an approach which when embraced allows for a greater level of support for disability experiences. How can we as a public space and organization reduce the experiences of disability that people have?"

REFERENCES

Brown, Freddy J., and Sarah Brown. 2016. *When Young People with Intellectual Disabilities and Autism Hit Puberty: A Parents' Q&A Guide to Health, Sexuality and Relationships.* London: Jessica Kingsley.

Campbell, Karolyn. 2019, November. Conversation with author.

Cooper, Kate, Laura G. E. Smith, and Ailsa J. Russell. 2018. "Gender Identity in Autism: Sex Differences in Social Affiliation with Gender Groups." *Journal of Autism and Developmental Disorders* 48, no. 12: 3995–4006. doi:10.1007/s10803-018-3590-1.

DH. 2019, November. Conversation with author.

Gentry, Tony, Richard Kriner, Adam Sima, Jennifer Mcdonough, and Paul Wehman. 2014. "Reducing the Need for Personal Supports among Workers with Autism

Using an iPod Touch as an Assistive Technology: Delayed Randomized Control Trial." *Journal of Autism and Developmental Disorders* 45, no. 3: 669–84. https://doi.org/10.1007/s10803-014-2221-8.

Gera, Emily. 2019, January 22. "Americans Spent More Than $43 Billion on Video Games in 2018." Variety. https://variety.com/2019/gaming/news/americans-spent-more-than-43-billion-on-video-games-in-2018-1203114642.

Ke, Fengfeng, and Jewoong Moon. 2018. "Virtual Collaborative Gaming as Social Skills Training for High-Functioning Autistic Children." *British Journal of Educational Technology* 49, no. 4: 728–41. https://doi.org/10.1111/bjet.12626.

Mann, Benjamin. 2019, December. Conversation with author.

Montes, Guillermo. 2016. "Children with Autism Spectrum Disorder and Screen Time: Results from a Large, Nationally Representative US Study." *Academic Pediatrics* 16, no. 2: 122–28. https://doi.org/10.1016/j.acap.2015.08.007.

"New on ADA.gov." n.d. ADA.gov homepage. Americans with Disabilities Act. Accessed December 3, 2019. https://ada.gov.

"OmniPage Ultimate." n.d. Nuance Software Store. Accessed December 18, 2019. http://www.nuancesoftwarestore.com/omnipage-ultimate.

Rogers-Whitehead, Carrie. 2018, September 11. "Utah Afterschool Network—What Is the Homework Gap? How Digital Inclusion Affects Your Students." UAN Pro Learning, Utah Afterschool Network. https://utahafterschool.org/utah-afterschool-blog/item/49-what-is-the-homework-gap-how-digital-inclusion-affects-your-students.

Sankardas, Sulata Ajit, and Jayashree Rajanahally. 2017. "iPad: Efficacy of Electronic Devices to Help Children with Autism Spectrum Disorder to Communicate in the Classroom." *Support for Learning* 32, no. 2: 144–57. https://doi.org/10.1111/1467-9604.12160.

Staff, TR. 2013, December 30. "The Death of Libraries?" *MIT Technology Review.* https://www.technologyreview.com/s/404030/the-death-of-libraries.

Stanford University. 2018, October 16. "Virtual Reality Can Help Make People More Empathetic." *Stanford News.* https://news.stanford.edu/2018/10/17/virtual-reality-can-help-make-people-empathetic.

Stiller, Anja, Jan Weber, Finja Strube, and Thomas Mößle. 2019. "Caregiver Reports of Screen Time Use of Children with Autism Spectrum Disorder: A Qualitative Study." *Behavioral Sciences* 9, no. 5: 56. https://doi.org/10.3390/bs9050056.

"VR Learning Tools to Help Individuals with Autism: We Are Leveraging the Power of Virtual Reality to Develop Social and Communication Tools for Individuals with Autism." n.d. Floreo. Accessed November 29, 2019. https://floreotech.com.

Wyatt, Danielle, and Dale Leorke. 2019, October 29. "Technology Hasn't Killed Public Libraries—It's Inspired Them to Transform and Stay Relevant." The Conversation. https://theconversation.com/technology-hasnt-killed-public-libraries-its-inspired-them-to-transform-and-stay-relevant-100900.

"ZoomText and Fusion." n.d. Zoomtext.com. Accessed December 18, 2019. https://www.zoomtext.com.

Library Collections and Resources

According to publisher Reclamation Press in 2017, "We discovered that less than one third of 1% of the 22 million books on Amazon are in anyway connected to any topic on disability. Since disabled people are at least 19% of the U.S. population, that's a huge gap" (Stewart, 2017). Libraries can help fill those gaps by having inclusive and targeted collections. This last chapter provides suggestions on books to order for both the community and for professional development. It also discusses inclusivity in publishing and collection development. Included at the end of this chapter is a list of resources for librarians to understand those with autism, make connections, and stay on top of conversations and trends.

PUBLISHERS

Inclusivity in collections often starts from the top—the publishers. Publishers put out titles based on public demand and knowledge. Although there are more large publishers creating titles, those books are typically not written by authors who are disabled. In 2015 a publisher of diverse books, Lee & Low, conducted a disability baseline survey of major publishers. The results of that survey found that 92 percent of publishing industry staff are nondisabled (Lee and Low, 2015).

Another issue with publishing is that despite many smaller publishers, the industry is dominated by the Big 5: Hatchette Book Group, HarperCollins, Macmillan Publishers, Penguin Random House, and Simon and Schuster. Those are the biggest five trade publishers in the United States, and it was estimated in 2015 that these companies own about 80 percent of the traditional book publishing market (McIlroy, 2016). While diverse books are published by the Big 5, it can make it harder for a neurodiverse or disabled author to break into mainstream publishing. This monopoly affects the whole marketplace of writers and readers. In an article by Vox in 2019 about the e-book revolution the author writes about the hold of the Big 5. Quoting an antitrust law professor the article states, "There used to be hundreds of publishing companies. They're now mostly owned by five." The Big 5 have publishing practices that make it difficult to be an independent publisher, and new author (Grady, 2019).

Marieke Nijkamp, founder of DiversifiYA, states, "When we look at the books published about disability, the vast majority are written by non-disabled authors. . . . And prioritizing non-disabled voices instead of normalizing disabled voices strongly (and most often, negatively) colors the way we think about disability" (Leary, 2018). By featuring books by disabled authors in their collections and displays (otherwise known as D lit), librarians can help promote diverse books and counter stereotypes about disability.

Another option for writers and librarians to collect and write diverse books is through the small or independent press. Instead of going with a mainstream publisher, or another traditional company that have gatekeepers to new writers and may lack a diverse staff, a writer can pursue a different route. Here are some non–Big 5 publishers that specialize in educating and featuring the experience of those with autism and other disabilities:

- *Oleb Books*. This publisher out of Minneapolis publishes stories by writers with disabilities.
- *Reclamation Press*. This small press publishes "wisdom from disability communities" as well as other books focused on the intersectionality of race, class, gender, and ability.
- *Jessica Kingsley Press*. A London-based publisher of academic nonfiction with a wide variety of autism and neurodiverse-related titles.
- *disAbilities Books Press*. This publishing house, created by a special needs attorney, has professional help titles and memoirs for parents, professionals, and caregivers.
- *Woodbine House*. This publishing house based in Maryland publishes special needs titles for teachers, parents, children, and professionals.

Self-Publishing

Bowker, an affiliate of ProQuest, reported the self-publishing industry in the United States from 2013 to 2018. In 2018 they reported that self-published print and e-books grew at a rate of 40 percent and showed "no signs of slowing down" (ProQuest, 2019). Like with traditional publishing, self-publishing is dominated by only three providers, accounting for over

90 percent of sales (ProQuest, 2019). But unlike traditional publishing, there are not as many gatekeepers and barriers to self-publishing as with going through a traditional trade publisher.

Self-published books are an option for writers with autism and libraries. disAbilities Books Press assisted parents and caregivers with self-publishing their own titles for seven years. These books, like *Voices from the Spectrum: Parents, Grandparents, Siblings, People with Autism, and Professionals Share Their Wisdom*, are not available on Amazon. These books share personal experiences, thoughts, and essays on more niche topics that may have not been selected by a more traditional publisher. Although libraries may have more difficulties collecting, ordering, and processing self-published books, they are a source for stories about the autism and disability experiences that may not ever sit on a bookstore shelf.

Accessible Publishing

New technologies have allowed the growth of accessible publishing. This is an approach and process of publishing and book design where the texts are made in different formats to assist with reading. This can mean larger or specialized fonts, Braille, e-books that can be magnified or automated, and screen readers. Accessible publishing also includes making materials readable across multiple platforms and devices.

The publishing industry was focused for many years on printing as many books as possible as cheaply as possible. This meant it did not make financial sense to make just a few items that were in Braille, or large print. But technologies have brought down these costs.

Bookshare is the largest online library of digital books for people who may struggle to read print materials. Schools can get accounts with Bookshare for free, and libraries can sign up with a fee to access their services. Individuals who qualify can also use the site at no cost. Although the website does not automatically qualify those with autism, it allows for those with comorbid conditions that affect reading print to potentially be members of Bookshare (Bookshare, 2020).

Part of making a library's collection inclusive is having materials that are accessible to those with varying disabilities. Does your library purchase e-books or e-audiobooks? Do you have a large print collection? For more information about accessible and assistive technology, see Chapter 8.

BOOK RECOMMENDATIONS

Many memoirs and books, including this one, are written by those who are close to, or have worked with people with autism. They are not written by authors who are #actuallyautistic. To find a searchable database of writers with disabilities, check out Disabled Writers at https://disabledwriters .com and follow the hashtag #actuallyautistic to read more of their voices.

There is controversy about memoirs being written about those with autism, typically parents. One boycott happened with the 2017 title, *To Siri with Love*, by Judith Newman. Newman has written about her son with autism in a *New York Times* column and put more of those experiences in that title. Some people saw the book as exploitative and uncaring of the boy's privacy. The hashtag #BoycottToSiri trended on Twitter (Frazier, 2017).

Librarians should be aware of controversies on this topic, and work to include books about autism written by those who have the diagnosis. Stories and memoirs of family focus the attention of the story on themselves, not necessarily the person with autism they are caring for. Geek Club Books has guidelines on their website for what they will recommend from neurotypical authors. Their guidelines can advise librarians when picking out titles that are inclusive and respectful:

- Books that do not advocate for finding a cure for autism.
- Scientific practices and treatments.
- No ableism—books that do not portray their characters as heroic for socializing and helping individuals who are disabled.
- Titles that make sure they have consent from the individuals before sharing personal information. This could include memoirs that are written with, rather than about, those with a disability.

Geek Club Books has an Autism Book Shop of recommended titles on Amazon (Geek Club Books, 2019).

Here are some suggestions of memoirs aimed at teens and adults with autism written by someone with autism:

Fiction

- *Queens of Geek* by Jen Wilde
- *On the Edge of Gone* by Corrine Duyvis
- Aspean series by Roy Dias
- *Mouse* by Richard Ford Burley
- *The Isle of Kern* by Jenny Bristol
- *The Orphan's Code* by C. R. R. Hillin
- *Underdogs* by Chris Bonnello

Nonfiction

- *Being Seen: Memoir of an Autistic Mother, Immigrant and Zen Student* by Anlor Davin

- *A Freshman Survival Guide for College Students with Autism Spectrum Disorders* by Haley Moss
- *Thinking in Pictures: My Life with Autism* by Temple Grandin
- *Fall Down 7 Times Get Up 8* by Naoki Higashida
- *The Reason I Jump: The Inner Voice of a Thirteen-Year-Old Boy with Autism* by Naoki Higashida
- *What Every Autistic Girl Wishes Her Parents Knew* by the Autism Women's Network
- *Unbroken: 13 Stories Starring Disabled Teens* by Marieke Nijkamp
- *Look Me in the Eyes* by John Elder Robinson
- *Raising Cubby: A Father and Son's Adventures with Asperger's, Trains, Tractors, and High Explosives* by John Elder Robinson
- Asperkids series by Jennifer Cook O'Toole
- *Twirling Naked in the Streets and No One Noticed: Growing Up with Undiagnosed Autism* by Jeannie Davide-Rivera
- *Why Does Daddy Always Look So Sad?* by Jude Morrow
- *Aspergirls: Empowering Females with Asperger Syndrome* by Rudy Simone
- *Asperger's on the Inside* by Michelle Vines
- *Everything You Need to Know from Autistics, Parents, and Professionals* edited by Shannon Des Roches Rosa
- *Come to Life! Your Guide to Self-Discovery* by Tom Iland
- *It's an Autism Thing . . . I'll Help You Understand It* by Emma Dalmayne

There are also a great many titles written by professionals, authors, and those who feature characters with autism (Geek Club Books, 2019). This is not an exhaustive list but includes well-reviewed titles that work to fairly represent those with autism.

Books for Young Children

- *Benji, the Bad Day, and Me* by Sally J. Pla
- *I Want to Be Like Poppin' Joe: A True Story Promoting Inclusion and Self-Determination* by Jo Meserve Mach
- *The Girl Who Thought in Pictures: The Story of Dr. Temple Grandin* by Julia Finley Mosca
- *Uniquely Wired: A Story about Autism and Its Gifts* by Julia Cook
- *All My Stripes: A Story for Children with Autism* by Shaina Rudolph
- *Really, Really Like Me* by Gretchen Leary (written and illustrated by two individuals on the autism spectrum)
- *The Quiet Bear* by Gretchen Leary (written by an individual with autism)
- *The Noah and Logan Children's Book Series* by Benjamin Kellogg (five volumes written by an individual with autism)

Fiction

- *Miracle Creek* by Angie Kim
- *The Boy Who Steals Houses* by C. G. Drews
- *The New Adventures of Jake Jetpulse* by Led Bradshaw
- *Mockingbird* by Kathryn Erskine
- *Anything but Typical* by Nora Raleigh Baskin
- *The Speed of Dark* by Elizabeth Moon
- *The Rosie Project* by Graeme Simsion
- *Marcelo in the Real World* by Francisco X. Stork
- *The Curious Incident of the Dog in the Night-Time* by Mark Haddon

Nonfiction

- *Beyond the Autistic Plateau—A Parent's Story and Practical Help with Autism* by Stephen Pitman
- *I Think I Might Be Autistic: A Guide to Autism Spectrum Disorder Diagnosis and Self-Discovery for Adults* by Cynthia Kim
- *An Asperger's Guide to Dating Neurotypicals: P.S. It's for Married Couples Too!* by J. R. Reed
- *Freaks, Geeks and Asperger Syndrome: A User Guide to Adolescence* by Luke Jackson
- *Ten Things Every Child with Autism Wishes You Knew* by Ellen Notbohm
- *Rain Man* by Leonore Fleischer and Kieran McGovern
- *NeuroTribes: The Legacy of Autism and the Future of Neurodiversity* by Steve Silberman

RESOURCES FOR LIBRARIANS

There are more resources than ever on the topic of autism spectrum disorder (ASD). Still, like other nonfiction and topical titles, librarians should make sure their collections and resources are up to date. Corey Seeman writes in *Library Journal,* "Autism today is practically a different condition than it was thought to be just 20 years ago. Early books, most notably Bruno Bettelheim's *The Empty Fortress* (1971), wrongly concluded that unloving, or 'refrigerator,' parents caused autism. Although that work is historically important, it would be damaging for someone to read it today. Public libraries, then, should look at tossing books published before the mid-1990s" (Seeman, 2003).

Most of the books recommended early are written since the 2000s. With the exception of certain memoirs and titles written by those with autism, librarians should look carefully at older books they have. Older books also use outdated or controversial terms like "handicapped" or "retarded" that are not in use today.

More recent nonfiction titles focus on the intersectionality of disability, race, gender, sexuality, and more. Here are some titles recommended by Karolyn Campbell (2019), executive director of the Disabled Rights Action Committee:

- *Crip Theory* by Robert McRuer
- *Extraordinary Bodies* by Rosemary Garland Thompson
- *Feminist, Queer, Crip* by Alison Kafer
- *A History of Disability* by Henri-Jaques Striker

There are also many organizations and websites that can assist librarians. Throughout this book many of them have been referenced. Check out the end of each chapter for more specifics.

- *ADAPT.* This nonprofit activist group has worked over forty years in areas of housing, health care, access, and more for those with disabilities. https://adapt .org
- *Libraries and Autism: We're Connected.* This site offers library-specific training, resources, grants, and more. http://www.librariesandautism.org /index.htm
- *Autistic Self Advocacy Network (ASAN).* This organization is run by and for autistic individuals. It has advocacy initiatives, trainings and resources. https://autisticadvocacy.org
- *Autism Citizen, Inc.* This nonprofit advocates for civil rights and liberties of individuals with autism. https://autismcitizen.org
- *U.S. Department of Health and Human Services.* This government site has resources data on ASD. Some of the statistics used in this book were from their Congressional Reports.
- *Asperger/Autism Network (AANE).* Adults on the spectrum are involved in all parts of this organization. It serves thousands of autistic adults and their family members, spouses, and friends. AANE provides both in-person and virtual services and works to represent the voices of those on the spectrum. https://www.aane.org
- *National Institute of Child Health and Human Development (NICHD).* The NICHD, renamed the Eunice Kennedy Shriver National Institute of Child Health and Human Development, was initially founded by John F. Kennedy and later approved and supported by the U.S. Congress. It focuses on birth to adulthood of human development, conducting research. It has information about therapies and intervention programs for persons with disabilities. https://www.nichd.nih.gov
- *University of Kentucky Guides.* The University of Kentucky has free trainings, resources, and suggestions for libraries working with those with autism. http://libguides.uky.edu/autismresources

- *Disability Compendium.* This compendium compiles various statistics through census data throughout the United States in a free guide. Some of the statistics in this book were found through the compendium. https://disabilitycompendium.org
- *Autism Society of America.* This nonprofit has run over fifty years advocating at the federal level and has featured voices of those with autism, like Temple Grandin on their board. https://www.autism-society.org
- *National Autistic Society (NAS).* This organization is focused on autism advocacy, programs, training, and treatment in the United Kingdom. https://www.autism.org.uk
- *Autism Canada/Autism Society of Canada.* This large nonprofit provides services, funding, education, and more to those on the autism spectrum. Their website states that they work to "see the potential for people living with autism" and "see and respect the person as an individual first." https://autismcanada.org
- *Centers for Disease Control and Prevention (CDC).* They have up-to-date data and statistics on autism free to the public. https://www.cdc.gov/ncbddd/autism/index.html
- *Autism Science Foundation.* This top-rated charity helps provide funding to scientists and institutions engaging in autism research. It also works to educate the public on ASD. https://autismsciencefoundation.org
- *Disability Visibility Project.* This podcast series features voices of those with disabilities on a variety of topics. https://disabilityvisibilityproject.com
- *National Association of Councils on Developmental Disabilities (NACDD).* This national organization administers the state and territorial developmental disability councils across the United States. Each state has their developmental disability council with resources and support. https://www.nacdd.org

Truly, patrons are the best resource for librarians about those with autism. Sit down with those on the spectrum and ask their advice. Include them on committees and advisory boards. Read books and articles with their voices. Don't assume that because you've just talked to one person with autism you know all about it. Rely on primary sources, not secondary. Go to the source—people who live every day with autism.

REFERENCES

Andrews, Joanna, Kristyn Roth, and Delancy Allred. 2019, September 24. "Home." Autism Society. https://www.autism-society.org.
"Autism Spectrum Disorder (ASD)." 2019, August 27. Centers for Disease Control and Prevention. https://www.cdc.gov/ncbddd/autism/index.html.
Autistic Self Advocacy Network. "Autistic Self Advocacy Network." Accessed November 3, 2019. https://autisticadvocacy.org.
"Books by Autistic Authors: Geek Club Books Author Interviews." n.d. Geek Club Books. Accessed December 24, 2019. https://geekclubbooks.com/autistic-authors.

Campbell, Karolyn. 2019, November. Conversation with author.

"Disability Visibility Project." 2019, June 24. Disability Visibility Project. https://disabilityvisibilityproject.com.

"The Diversity Baseline Survey." n.d. The Diversity Baseline Survey, Lee & Low Books. Accessed December 24, 2019. https://www.leeandlow.com/about-us/the-diversity-baseline-survey.

Frazier, Andrea. 2017, December 4. "People Are Super Pissed about This Book a Mom Wrote about Her Son with Autism." Romper. https://www.romper.com/p/people-want-to-boycott-to-siri-with-love-saying-it-invades-the-privacy-of-a-boy-with-autism-6768968.

"Free Our People!" n.d. ADAPT. Accessed December 24, 2019. https://adapt.org.

Grady, Constance. 2019, December 23. "The 2010s Were Supposed to Bring the eBook Revolution. It Never Quite Came." Vox. https://www.vox.com/culture/2019/12/23/20991659/ebook-amazon-kindle-ereader-department-of-justice-publishing-lawsuit-apple-ipad.

"Home." n.d. Woodbine House. Accessed December 24, 2019. http://www.woodbinehouse.com.

"Home Page." n.d. Jessica Kingsley Publishers. Accessed December 24, 2019. https://www.jkp.com/usa.

Leary, Alaina. 2018, January 10. "Publishing Has Failed Autistic & Disabled People—Here's How to Fix It." Bustle. https://www.bustle.com/p/why-the-publishing-industry-needs-to-be-more-inclusive-of-autistic-disabled-people-7705640.

Libraries and Autism: We're Connected. Accessed December 24, 2019. http://www.librariesandautism.org/index.htm.

McIlroy, Thad. 2016, August 8. "What the Big 5's Financial Reports Reveal." Book Business. https://www.bookbusinessmag.com/post/big-5-financial-reports-reveal-state-traditional-book-publishing.

"National Association of Councils on Developmental Disabilities." 2019, August 7. NACDD. https://www.nacdd.org.

Oleb Books. https://olebbooks.com.

ProQuest. "News 2020—Self-Publishing Grew 40 Percent in 2018, New Report Reveals." Bowker. Accessed January 31, 2020. http://www.bowker.com/news/2020/Self-Publishing-Grew-40-Percent-in-2018-New-Report—Reveals.html.

"Read Your Way." Bookshare. Accessed January 31, 2020. https://www.bookshare.org/cms.

"Research Guides: Autism Resources: Home." n.d. Home—Autism Resources—Research Guides at University of Kentucky. Accessed December 24, 2019. http://libguides.uky.edu/autismresources.

Seeman, Corey. 2003. "Sending Postcards from the Airport." *Library Journal* 128, no. 12: 45.

Stewart, Christy L., Reclamation Press, and Reclamation Press Post. 2017, August 15. "Why Disability-Centered Publishers Are Needed." Reclamation Press. https://www.reclapress.com/launching-reclamation-press.

U.S. Census Bureau. 2017. American Community Survey, 1-Year Estimates, American FactFinder, Table B18120. Accessed August 1, 2019. https://factfinder.census.gov.

"Welcome to Disabled Writers." n.d. Disabled Writers. Accessed December 24, 2019. https://disabledwriters.com.

Appendix

Programs to Use in Your Library

Author's Note: This Appendix has resources, program outlines, and practical suggestions for creating, adapting, and/or implementing library programs for adults and teens with autism. Most of the programs included in this Appendix are ones I have personally implemented in my own programs. As the saying goes, if you've met one person with autism, you've met one person with autism. The programs listed may appeal to certain individuals on the spectrum more than others. The only way to truly find out is to try them out! Over the years I found what worked best and repeated those activities. This Appendix includes some of the favorites. You can also find some of the most popular programs scattered throughout the rest of the book.

In creating these programs, I leaned heavily on the parents who attended my programs, books, the autism nonprofit community, and the research of other librarians, particularly Tricia Twarogowski. Tricia has published some of the best articles on sensory programs in the Association for Library Service to Children and was always more than willing to talk (Twarogowski, 2009). When I started researching this topic, Tricia's work was one of the few things that I discovered in my searches. She paved the way for others and was invaluable as I got started with library work for those with autism back in 2010. As you develop your own programs, do not do it alone. There are many caregivers, therapists, librarians, and advocates working in this area who will more than likely advise and help.

Most of the programs described in this Appendix were developed for the people who came to my library. Autism is a spectrum, and the attendees that typically came to my programs were those who were more severely affected by their diagnosis. I had regular attendees who were nonverbal, would come with a full-time caregiver, and/or had mobility concerns. This may not be the same makeup of people who attend your programs. But these programs can be adapted to fit their needs.

This Appendix is divided into broad categories of activities and program ideas:

- Music Programs
- STEM Programs
- Geek Programs
- Craft Programs
- Reading Dogs
- Organizing Autism Outreach

I was fortunate to have a regular volunteer in all of my sensory programs, the amazing Chris Kamlowsky, to whom this book is dedicated. Chris would joke that "we throw a bunch of things at the wall and see what sticks" when running our program. Her statement is accurate; we were always experimenting and trying something new. Yes, not everything stuck, but the process weeded out the most popular activities, and was fun along the way. Throw a few of these program ideas at the wall; I'm sure you'll get at least one that sticks!

MUSIC PROGRAMS

Music was a regular part of my sensory programs for children to adults. Music played when everyone entered, to signal transitions from one activity to another, and during open play/social time. I remember how music particularly transfixed one adult attendee who was mostly nonverbal. Although he could not speak much, he loved dancing and music. He would lean in very close to the CD player so he could listen as shown in Photo A.1.

In an article published in the *Scientific American Mind* in 2015, the topic of music therapy for those with autism spectrum disorder is discussed.

> Perhaps the most fascinating interplay between music and the brain lies in the case files of people with autism spectrum disorder . . . up to 30 percent of people with autism cannot make the sounds of speech at all; many have limited vocabulary of any kind, including gesture.

PHOTO A.1. Program participant listening to music in program.

One of the peculiarities of the neurobiology of autism is the overdevelopment of short-range brain connections. As an apparent consequence, children with autism tend to focus intensely on the fine details of sensory experience, such as the varying textures of different fabrics or the precise sound qualities emitted by appliances such as a refrigerator or an air conditioner. And this fascination with sound may account for the many anecdotal reports of children with autism who thoroughly enjoy making and learning music.

The positive response to music opens the way to treatments that can help children with autism engage in activities with other people, acquiring social, language and motor skills as they do. Music also activates areas of the brain that relate to social ways of thinking. When we listen to music, we often get a sense of the emotional states of the people who created it and those who are playing it. By encouraging children with autism to imagine these emotions, therapists can help them learn to think about other people and what they might be feeling. (Thompson and Schlaug, 2015)

Music is more than a library program; it can be therapeutic. Alternate between upbeat and slow songs or "sad" or "happy" songs and ask the participants to express how they feel. Move music from background music to the centerpiece of your program.

SAMPLE PROGRAM IDEA: MUSIC ON TABLETS

If you have access to devices like a tablet or smartphones, there are many different musical apps available for free. When searching for musical apps, look at ones targeted for children; some of the others have a higher learning curve and may require the ability to read music. The activity is less about teaching how to make music than encouraging socialization, teamwork, and motor skills.

Materials:

- One device for every one or two participants. By sharing the devices, this can encourage teamwork and communication.
- Installed music apps.

    Note: The apps I used in my programs were available on iPad minis. They were Kids Piano Sound Touch and Storybots. The Kids Piano app was one where you could click different notes on a virtual keyboard to create different instrument sounds. The Storybots app includes these colorful robots that when you press them make different sounds. You can play and compose simple songs by touching the robots.

    Note: Storybots is part of a large franchise, which has won Emmys on Netflix. There are many Storybots songs and resources available for educators online: https://wwww.storybots.com. Although their classroom set was not available when I did this program, you can now request it from their website. It has free educational books, videos, and games (Storybots, 2020).

Instructions:

1. Assign devices to the participants.
2. Allow them 5–10 minutes to test out the apps and play.
3. Pick a simple song. I suggest a nursery rhyme like "Mary Had a Little Lamb" or "Peas Porridge Pot," which are easier to follow. Another fun and recognizable song is "We Will Rock You" by Queen, which can encourage them to stay on rhythm.
4. Demonstrate how to play the song. If possible, project your device so others can see what you are doing.
5. Encourage them to repeat the song on their devices.

    Note: With everyone playing at once it may be noisy, and some who have sensory concerns may need to choose a corner of the room. If headphones are available, you can provide them so it's not as much of an issue. If you do use headphones in these programs, remember to wipe down the headphones before storing them.

Other easy-to-use music apps include:

- Bandimal
- Musical Me
- Toca Band
- Musitude

SAMPLE PROGRAM IDEA: SHAKERS

Shakers are a staple of library story times and an activity those of every age and ability can enjoy. This type of shaker is inexpensive, easy to make, and ideal for both movement and music.

Materials:

- Paper plates. Buy the inexpensive white plates that are easy to bend.
- Stapler.
- Beads, beans, corn, or other item that makes noise.
- Colored streamers. You can also use tissue paper or ribbon.
- Markers, crayons, or other items to decorate.

Instructions:

1. Give everyone a paper plate. Distribute the coloring supplies, noise-making items, and streamers among the participants.
2. Take a handful of beans, beads, etc., and place them on one half of the paper plate.
3. Place several colored streamers or tissue paper on the half of the paper plate with the beans. Make sure most of the paper is outside the plate.
4. Bend the paper plate over the beans/beads.
5. Staple the edges of the paper plate together so the circle of the plate turns into a semicircle. Make sure the space between the staples is close so any beans/beads don't escape.
6. Decorate the outside of the plate.
7. Shake, swirl, bounce, twist, and move your plate to the rhythm.

Other ideas for shakers:

- Use a plastic bottle with a cap. Put in your noise makers and you're ready to shake.
- Put small items in Easter eggs and tape shut.
- Fill a cardboard or toilet paper tube full of items and staple shut.

Other music program ideas:

- *Garage Band.* This is a free software available on Apple Devices. Although more complicated than the apps listed above, it can be a great way to compose music.
- *Musical Freeze Tag.* Play an upbeat song, and when the music stops you have to freeze. Two songs in particular that incorporate freezing are Jim Gill's "Spin Again" and "Jumping and Counting" (Gill, 2020).

- *Drumming.* Put on a song and encourage drumming to the beat. You don't have to have actual drums for this but can use pots, bowls, the table, and more.

STEM PROGRAMS

STEM stands for science, technology, engineering, and math. The activities in this section demonstrate some principles from sciences like chemistry and physics. The STEM activities included in this section are simple for busy librarians and participants who may have mobility, sensory, and other concerns. Technology-specific program are described in Chapter 8.

STEM Programs in a Box

Librarians are busy and don't always have time to plan and collect all the things needed for a STEM program. When I ran STEM programs for those with autism, I relied on kits and boxes made internally and externally. There may be organizations near you that allow free or low-cost checkout of all the materials you need for an engaging STEM program. One popular program-in-a-box I ran was getting furs, bones, shells, and other items from the Utah Natural History Museum. The items were laid out and identified, and the participants could touch and feel the different textures. The Natural History Museum's teaching toolboxes were free to educators; all they asked is that you picked up and dropped the kit off on time (Teaching Toolboxes, 2020).

Here are some other organizations that offer classroom kits:

- Science museums, like the Smithsonian or the Museum of Aviation Foundation.
- Universities.
- 4H Clubs. Some 4H clubs have kits available for borrowing. Other kits are available at a low cost on the national website at https://shop4-h.org/collections/educational-kits (Educational Kits, 2020).

SAMPLE PROGRAM IDEA: VACUUM PACKED

This simple and short STEM activity can demonstrate the properties of a vacuum. Pick a participant who feels comfortable with deep pressure and likes items like weighted blankets. Warn any attendees with hearing sensitivities that the vacuum can get loud. Some participants may not like the sound of the vacuum, but there are some who may appreciate it. I had an attendee who would often volunteer to vacuum up at the end of the program. He enjoyed the feel of the vibration when he would push it around. The sound the vacuum made was a white noise that was calming. We were more than happy to let him vacuum all he wanted!

Materials:

- Large garbage or leaf bag
- Tank vacuum

Instructions:

1. Ask for a volunteer to be vacuum packed. It will not hurt them, but if someone is uncomfortable with tight closing or some pressure it may be uncomfortable.

2. Have the volunteer step into the bag, and make sure the bag does not go over the person's face, or that there are any holes in it.

3. Turn on the tank vacuum and place it near the volunteer's stomach. Do not have the vacuum hose touch their clothes or the bag.

4. Turn on the vacuum and watch it tighten around the body. If done correctly, the volunteer should not be able to move at all.

5. Explain the science behind the experiment: everything that takes up space is matter. Even air, which you can't see, is still matter and has pressure. You can see the space air takes up by blowing up a balloon or sucking the air out of the garbage bag. By sucking air out of the vacuum, it decreases the air pressure. No air is pushing against the sides of the garbage bag (Rogers-Whitehead, 2015).

SAMPLE PROGRAM IDEA: PLAY WITH SAND

Sensory programs can entertain and calm at all ages and abilities. I have used them from toddlers to adults. One fun, albeit messy, sensory activity is using sand. This activity with sand demonstrates STEM principles, and there are additional options on using sand in programs.

Hydrophobic Sand STEM Activity

Materials:

- Sand

  Note: When purchasing sand, you'll want to find a product advertised as "play sand." Play sand is washed and sometimes has products like silica removed. Silica can be toxic if inhaled in excess. You can also look for products that advertise their sand as silica-free or specifically labeled "craft sand" found in places like Michaels. In addition to craft stores, you can purchase sand at hardware stores like The Home Depot.

- Fabric protector spray (like Scotch Guard)
- Aluminum foil
- Water

Instructions:

1. Lay sand out in a thick layer on foil. Spray liberally with the fabric protector.

2. Shuffle sand around and spray again until well coated.

3. Let dry for a few minutes.

4. Fill a clear glass container with water and drop the treated sand into the water.

5. The sand should clump and form shapes. The spray coats the sand causing it to repel the water and stay dry.

6. Explain the science behind the experiment. This activity demonstrates the hydrophobic effect, which is the tendency of nonpolar substances (i.e., where there is a symmetrical arrangement of polar bonds) to clump together and push away water molecules. This hydrophobic effect is responsible for the mixture of oils and waters, also demonstrated in the later activity of creating sensory jars. Oil and fats are also nonpolar substances. The hydrophobic effect is essential for life through cell biology.

7. Consider asking these questions to encourage self-reflection: Why does the sand behave this way? What would happen if you didn't coat the sand with spray first before putting it in the water? (Rogers-Whitehead, 2016)

Other activities with sand:

- *Sand sensory table.* Using play or craft sand put various items like rocks, plastic figures, and digging tools into a long sandbox, bin, or table.

- *Create moon sand.* Moon sand purchased in a craft store can be expensive. Moon, also called kinetic sand, is similar to the hydrophobic sand in the STEM activity. It clumps and sticks together. There are various different recipes to create moon sand that can save on money and provide an entertaining sensory activity.

- *DIY sand Zen garden.* Using a sand sensory table or bin, create a calming Zen-like garden. You can purchase portable Zen gardens, or you can create your own. Some of them are created in shadow boxes or clear glass bowls but can also be created in just about any container with a wide opening. They need play or craft sand, and you can also add a few drops of essential oils to the sand for a relaxing scent. Include a sand rake, which can be a small beach toy or even a fork with bent tines. Include a few smooth rocks and faux plants. Encourage the participants to take the sand rake and create patterns in the sand. This type of play is slower and calmer (Admin, 2019).

SAMPLE PROGRAM IDEA: RAIN CLOUDS IN A JAR

This was a popular STEM activity we repeated because it not only was easy to run, but participants wanted to do it again. It teaches basic weather science concepts, and the shaving cream can provide an optional sensory experience.

Materials:

- Clear jars or glasses.

  Note: I suggest a wide-mouthed Mason jar.
- Food coloring.
- Shaving cream.

  Note: Do not spend much money on this, and buy more than you think you need because shaving cream can be used for other sensory activities. Go to the Dollar Store and buy their simple Barbasol brand.
- Small plastic bowls, about one for every participant
- Eye droppers, one for every person
- Pitcher with water

Instructions:

1. Fill the Mason jars about halfway to three-quarters full of water.
2. Add different food coloring to the small plastic bowls. Create a concentrated mix.
3. Have the participants cover the top of their Mason jar with shaving cream.
4. Fill up the eye dropper with one of the colors from the small plastic bowl.
5. Gently and slowly drip the food coloring on top of the shaving cream on the jar.
6. Watch the cloud "rain" with the colored droplets.
7. Allow everyone to experiment with different colors and amounts until the water in the jar is a solid color. Then you can pour out the shaving cream and water and start again.
8. Explain the science behind the experiment. Water can be a liquid, solid, and gas, also called water vapor. Water vapor gets into our atmosphere through a process called evaporation. As water vapor rises into the atmosphere, it cools down and forms tiny water droplets through a process called condensation. The droplets turn into clouds, our shaving cream. As the droplets make bigger and heavier clouds, they get too heavy to stay up in the atmosphere. This is when rain, snow, or hail falls to the earth (Rogers-Whitehead, 2015).

GEEK PROGRAMS

Like many other librarians, I am a self-proclaimed geek. Over the years some of my favorite parts of librarianship were creating small- and large-scale geek programs for all ages and abilities. For those programs with autism I consistently included geek elements and themes. Over time the participants began to expect this, and I would get questions like "When is Spider-Man coming back?" I regularly had cosplayers visit the program, and each year we would have an annual Superhero Day during Autism Awareness Month in April.

Before adding these geek elements to your programs to those with autism, survey them about their favorite characters, stories, TV shows, and movies. Tailor your geek programs to what they watch and follow. More geek programs are included in earlier chapters of this book, and if you wanted a deeper dive into geek programs at the library for teens, read my 2018 book with Rowman & Littlefield, *Teen Fandom and Geek Programing: A Practical Guide for Librarians*.

Hosting Cosplayers at the Library

Cosplay, or "costume play," is when participants wear and often create costumes, weapons, and other accessories to represent a specific character. This can be a character from books, TV, anime, video games, or one they came up with themselves. The art of cosplay has grown rapidly with geek culture. Anyone can cosplay, although some have more experience with it.

I would regularly have cosplayers at my sensory programs over the years. Only a very few cosplayers do it for money; most dress up for charity. They come out and interact, take pictures, and talk at events with schools, nonprofits, and libraries. The caregivers and cosplayers said it was one of their favorite programs. If you want to bring in cosplayers to your library, here are some tips I've learned over the years:

- Many local cosplay groups are formed from volunteers and may not be very tightly run. They may not have a website, only a Facebook or Instagram page. Sometimes the groups are only found through word of mouth. Give yourself some extra time to contact and coordinate these groups with your library.

- Treat cosplayers kindly and respectfully. They are taking time out of their day to come to your library and are not being reimbursed.

- Give plenty of notice before booking. Some more organized and in-demand groups book out months in advance, particularly for the summer.

- Send out a reminder of the library program a week in advance.

- Provide shade and water if you are having your library program outside. Some costumes, particularly ones that are made out of foam or metal, get very hot.

- Take pictures of the cosplayers at your event and tag and share the pictures. Help promote their group to other libraries and organizations.

- Provide a place for storage and changing. Many cosplayers change at the location and need room and time to put on their outfits (Rogers-Whitehead, 2018).

When cosplayers came to my programs with those with autism, I would tell them the population they were working with and encourage them to give them space. Over the years I had a few participants who felt nervous around the cosplayers since they were unfamiliar or the program room got loud with the extra people. Never push for interactions and allow a quiet space in the room if someone needs a break.

SAMPLE PROGRAM IDEA: BOX ROBOTS

This is a simple activity with little prep that became a favorite in my teen anime club. It became an annual tradition to have a box robot afternoon. This program outline has been adapted for those on the autism spectrum.

Materials:

- Cardboard boxes of all shapes and sizes. Consider finding boxes with thinner cardboard because the thick cardboard is hard to cut. Also, gather boxes from other items such as shoes, cereal, and tissues.
- Tape. Buy the plain gray duct tape in bulk because it is expensive. Also, consider buying some painters tape for decoration and binding together lighter materials.
- Scissors. Safety scissors will not cut boxes very well, so you'll want something thicker and more heavy duty. For those with mobility issues, have the caregivers handle the scissors.
- (Optional) Box cutters. This will make cutting the box easier, but they are very sharp so watch them closely.
- (Optional) Buttons, bottle caps, empty plastic bottles, and other decorations for the robot.
- (Optional) Markers and crayons to decorate the robot.

Instructions:

1. Set out one table with the decorations and another with scissors and tape for constructing the robot.
2. Place the different size boxes on the floor near the tables.
3. Encourage the participants to create their own robot. Show them examples of what this could look like. On Instructables there are many robot costumes with instructions to get you inspired: https://www.instructables.com/id/Robot-Costumes (Bulnick, 2020).
4. Give a time limit to create the robot, and tell the participants they can show off their robot to the group at the end if they are interested.
5. This program is messy, so allow a few minutes at the end for people to pick up, put supplies away, and recycle any leftover cardboard (Rogers-Whitehead, 2017).

Variations on Box Robots Program

- *Make a human robot.* Assign a person to be the "robot," and everyone turns that person into a robot—putting cardboard around the legs, making a helmet, etc.

- *Robot fight.* Divide the group into two teams, each creating their own human robot. Make it a competition on who can assemble the best-constructed robot. You can give the human robot tasks such as "jump on one leg for 5 seconds" or "crawl under a table" or have them race each other across the room.
- *Robots from fandoms.* This activity can be tailored to a specific robot, like Transformers, or a mecha anime like Gundam or Gurren Lagaan. Show examples of robots from the fandom and include supplies on how to make those specific robots. Play an episode of the fandom while they are working on constructing the robot.
- *Mini robots.* Instead of larger human robots, encourage small robots with shoe boxes, small gift packages, and more.
- *Valentines robots.* Many schools ask their students to make a box for holding Valentines cards. Create a "Love Bot" with red, pink, and white boxes and paper. Make sure the "Love Bot" has a place for cards to go inside. Include some paper for participants to make their own Valentines for others.

SAMPLE PROGRAM IDEA: SUPERHERO DAY

Each year in April I would spend extra time planning and marketing sensory programs in celebration with Autism Awareness Month. In your community during April you will typically see more autism-themed events, fund-raisers, activities, and more. This provides opportunities for partnerships and cross promotions. One program I would time during April is an annual superhero day. Once a year for three years we would have a superhero party celebrating all the "superpowers" of autism because our differences make us "super."

Materials:

- Superhero shield. Create a superhero shield with card stock in bright colors. Provide markers and crayons to decorate the shield.
- Colorful décor. Pick bold colors of purple, red, blue, green, and yellow for tablecloths and streamers.
- Caution tape.
- Cosplayers. You cannot have a superhero party without superheroes! Two to three months in advance recruit cosplayers in superhero costumes to your party. See more advice on getting cosplayers to your library above.

Instructions:

1. Create at least three stations with different superhero activities. Cosplayers can be at each station to help out the participants.
2. When the attendees arrive, have them first go get their superhero shield and name. Use a Superhero Name Generator online, or simply let them pick what they want their superhero name to be. They can decorate their paper shield with their superhero name.

Note: Instead of a shield, you can also provide a cape. There are capes that can be purchased online, or if someone has some sewing skills a cape can be made with about ½–1 yard of fabric. Although more expensive, if you use fabric like polyester, felt, or fleece, the ends will not fray.

3. One popular superhero station was an obstacle course. With caution tape a part of the room was blocked off with chairs, tables, and other furniture. The attendees were encouraged to navigate through the obstacle course without touching the table. Another type of obstacle course is balancing and can be done simply by putting tape on the floor and having them walk on the tape without "falling" off.

4. Choose your own additional superhero stations. See below for more ideas.

5. Make sure to include a quiet area in your superhero program. This program can be more crowded and frenetic and may require some participants to need a break. You can ask one of the cosplayer volunteers to be in that quiet area with books for an impromptu story time.

6. Provide time at the end of the program for people to take pictures with the cosplayers. Also, consider creating a group activity with the cosplayers. For example, one time we did a game where they had to keep balloons in the air.

Variations on Superhero Day Program

- *Superhero cuffs.* Consider making a craft station part of your superhero day. There are many different options for this theme of craft. One simple idea is superhero cuffs, like the gold cuffs Wonder Woman has. You'll want empty toilet paper rolls, stickers, markers, crayons, and colored paper. Simply cut the toilet paper roll in half and decorate it. You can also use card stock for the cuffs instead of toilet paper rolls, but the toilet paper rolls are already sized.

- *Superheroes with disAbilities.* Consider featuring or talking about particular superheroes whose differences and disabilities make them even stronger. For example, Daredevil is blind but it enhances his other senses to superhero-level abilities. Two superheroes who struggle with mobility are Professor X from the X-Men who is in wheelchair and Batgirl who was paralyzed from the waist down.

SAMPLE PROGRAM IDEA: ANIME ART CLASS

Anime art refers to the unique and stylized two- and three-dimensional animation and illustration that originated in Japan in the twentieth century. Anime art can also be considered cartoon animation created by a Japanese artist, in Japan or for a Japanese audience. Anime art includes all subject matter and is drawn with slender arms and legs, exaggerated expressions, and large eyes, and the drawings are more elaborate than cartoons. Any anime fan, even nonfans, can easily recognize it in movies, shows, artwork, visual novels, manga, games, and much more.

This program demonstrates on free image editing software, GIMP, that attendees can use at home or in the library to create and/or edit anime-style art.

Materials:

- Indoor space set up classroom style.
- Projector.
- Computer connected to the projector.
- Internet access.
- GNU Image Manipulation Program (GIMP) downloaded on computers. This is a free and open source image editor that has existed since the 1990s (GIMP, 2020). https://www.gimp.org.

Optional: Selection of manga and manga drawing books; pens, pencils, markers, and paper to sketch design before creating digitally; tablet or laptop for each participant.

Instructions:

1. Explain what anime art is and what makes it unique. Show examples and ask the participants to share their favorite examples of this art style. Some examples of this art style created by mostly non-Japanese amateurs can be found on deviantart.com.
2. Provide paper and drawing tools to sketch out designs for anime art.
3. Using the free GIMP software, a librarian will demonstrate how to use the software to make anime art.
4. Allow the participants to experiment with the software. Allow them to print out and/or save their designs on a USB if using library computers.

Other free software with similar functions as GIMP include:

- DAZ Studio
- Canva
- Krita.org
- Inkscape

Geeky Apps and Online Resources

Geek and fandom communities are very active online and have created a wealth of free resources and information. Here are some resources to reference and inspire for your own geeky and/or STEM programs:

- *3D printing geek templates.* Many fans have created geeky templates for 3D printing and shared them for free online. Check out the sites—Pinshape,

Thingiverse, YouMagine, TinkerCAD, and SketchUp—for some free templates (Rogers-Whitehead, 2018).

- *Animation.* You do not need to be an expert coder or graphic designer to create your own animated videos (Rogers-Whitehead, 2018). Some free sites include:
  - *CreaToon.* 2D animations.
  - *Pencil2D.* Traditional hand-drawn animations.
  - *Blender.* This is a public collaborative project for beginners to professionals. It has a free and paid version.
- *Visual novels.* Visual novels are interactive games, originating in Japan and typically using anime-style art. They include a text-based story, like a Choose Your Own Adventure novel. They are very popular in the anime fandom as well with other geeky fans. For visual novel fans, consider creating a library program introducing some visual novel software. You can even pick up some simple coding through this process. Some popular visual novel creation sites include:
  - *Ren'Py.* Free, but requires some basic coding skills.
  - *TyranoBuilder.* This software is drag and drop with an easy-to-use interface but comes at a cost.
  - *Visual Novel Maker.* This software is pricier but includes more options and art. It's aimed at more advanced creators.
- *Anime Music Videos (AMVs).* Anime Music Videos are edited anime clips set to music. They are very popular and have a devoted fanbase. A geeky STEM program could be teaching the basics of making your own AMV (Rogers-Whitehead, 2018). Some sources for creating your own AMVs include:
  - *Audacity.* This is a free and open source software that allows audio editing.
  - *YouTube.* A popular choice for editing and uploading AMVs. It includes some basic video editing software with an account.
  - *AnimeMusicVideos.org.* Besides YouTube, this is the biggest repository of AMVs to watch and get inspired. It also has forums to provide help and troubleshoot.

SAMPLE PROGRAM IDEA: FANFICTION WRITERS GROUP

Fanfiction are stories written about settings, plots, and characters found in TV, books, movies, video games, and pop culture. Fanfiction involves all genres and can involve multiple fandoms. Some writers use existing characters or create original characters (OC) written into their favorite fandoms. Fanfiction is written by all ages and across ability levels. Providing a safe space through a Fanfiction Writer's Group can encourage literacy, and new friendships through the love of the same characters and stories.

Materials:

- Indoor space set up with chairs at tables

  Optional: Snacks and a place for participants to put out their favorite books from the library on display. Set out paper and pencils for people to take notes. Consider facilitating or setting up an online group to keep the fanfiction discussions going outside the library.

Instructions:

A Fanfiction Writer's Group can be as simple or as complicated as you want it. It can simply be a place for writers to gather and talk about what they're working on and getting feedback from other writers. Or it can have specific activities each meeting.

Some ideas for fanfiction program ideas include:

- *Badfic.* This term refers to stories that are deliberately written badly. Members can be challenged to write their worst possible story or find the worst fanfiction story they've ever read and share it (Rogers-Whitehead, 2018).
- *Flashfic.* A flashfic is similar to a timed essay, where there's only so much time to write on a particular prompt. For example, you could ask the group to take 20 minutes to design a character or pick a setting that they must create a story. You could also provide a writing prompt—there is a subreddit called r/Writing Prompts that has literally thousands of prompts for writers.
- *Group story.* Start with a writing prompt; then go around the room and ask the attendees to add two or three sentences to the story. Then rotate to the next person until you have a complete, although probably nonsensical, story everyone wrote together.

CRAFT PROGRAMS

There are so many library craft program ideas out there. When creating my own crafts, I would frequently look to see what other libraries, bloggers, Pinterest moms, and others have done. The parents and caregivers who attended my sensory programs would also give me ideas and share resources they had used at home. Here is a small selection of craft ideas for autism programs that can be used with different ages and abilities. When creating craft programs for those with autism, keep in mind mobility issues. Sometimes pencils, scissors, and small objects can be hard to grip. There are also those who are nonverbal so do not simply explain how to make the craft, show, and put out an example to touch and examine. Get volunteers and the parents and caregivers in your program to guide and walk through the activities. Although some participants may need additional help, others may need you to get out of the way. Allow your program attendees to try out the crafts without stepping in. Let them experiment and try it out.

SAMPLE PROGRAM IDEA: MURAL ART

Offering collaborative art projects encourages teamwork and socialization between the artists. When drawing you have to make sure to leave space for others. You have to wait your turn and share the supplies. You also have to communicate together to make the piece cohesive. It is very satisfying after the hard work and the artists step back to see the final project.

When running my programs for those with autism, I would frequently tie in collaborative art projects. Here is a joint mural (Photo A.2) for a Star Wars themed program.

Materials:

- *Butcher paper.* Butcher paper is designed for handling oil or water when cooking. It is sturdier than average craft paper. Get the longer size, at least 24 inches tall.

  Note: Although a roll of butcher paper can be more expensive, it lasts a very long time and can be used in a variety of ways. For example, butcher paper is a substitute for tablecloths.

- *Markers, crayons, or paint.* Choose your medium depending on the activity. For paint, either have the mural outside and/or put paper around the mural and below it for drips.

- *Painter's tape.* This adheres the butcher paper to a surface to paint or draw. It also removes easily so the paper is not ruined. If taping a mural to an indoor wall, make a thick frame around the mural to protect from markers/crayons going outside the edge of the paper.

PHOTO A.2. Collaborative Star Wars mural.

Instructions:

- Create the blank canvas by adhering the paper to a wall or table.
- Set the supplies for drawing near the paper.
- Give your instructions on what you would like the mural to be. Then step aside and let the participants work. Only intervene if you feel someone is being excluded, there is pushing, or the art is going outside the bounds of the paper.

Mural ideas:

- Create a scene or setting.
- Draw part of an object/person/scene and ask them to complete and fill in the rest.
- Finger paint, no brushes allowed.
- Create a pointillism mural. Pointillism is the art of painting with small dots of color. This can be done with markers but is easily created with art dot markers. These types of markers are also ideal for those with mobility concerns.

SAMPLE PROGRAM IDEA: PAPER WREATH

This is a more time-consuming craft activity, but the time needed creates an opportunity for social interaction. Other positives are that it is inexpensive and adaptable to different holidays and seasons. In addition, the repetitive motions of making the wreath have similar health benefits to knitting crafts described in Chapter 6.

Materials:

- Wire hanger for each wreath.
- Tissue paper cut into rectangles about 4–5 inches in length and 1½ to 2 inches in width. You can decide to do one color of tissue paper or various colors. Different colors can be for different occasions like using only white makes a winter wreath while orange and black would be a Halloween wreath.

  Note: Instead of tissue paper you can make a literary-themed wreath with pages from books. If you do decide to cut up books, consider thinner paper, such as onion-skin paper found in older texts or Bibles, which is ideal.

- Optional: Include embellishments like ribbon, spray glitter, pinecones, sticker jewels, fake flowers, etc.

Instructions:

1. Stretch the clothes hanger to make it circular with the hook at the top.
2. Stack your tissue paper about ten sheets high. Then cut the tissue paper into rectangles the desired size.

3. Selecting an individual tissue piece, pinch then crimp at its center. Then twist at the middle around the wire, securing the tissue to the wire.

4. Continue crimping and twisting tissues on the hook against each other. Press them together firmly to make sure the wreath looks full. Continue crimping and twisting until the whole circle of the wire is covered in tissue paper.

5. Add any embellishments to the tissue paper. Note that the tissue paper is fragile and should be handled delicately.

Other variations of paper wreaths:

• Use a round Styrofoam frame instead of the wire hanger. Poke holes close together in the Styrofoam and put a dot of hot glue in each hole. With the tissue paper pieces twist them so there is a point at the end. Then place the tissue paper into the hole with the hot glue (Dann, 2016).

• Use wrapping paper instead of tissue paper for a holiday-themed wreath.

• Instead of stretching the wire hanger in a circle, make a heart for a Valentines-themed wreath.

Adult Coloring Books

Adult coloring books moved from a niche to global trend in 2013, and a big business for many craft and bookstores. These detailed and intricate coloring books became a past time for entertainment or calming. The American Art Therapy Association supports the use of coloring books for self-care (Blackburn and Chamley, 2016).

Librarians have offered programming around coloring books as the trend grew. Sometimes this is passive programming, such as putting out the books on tables at the library or as part of another program. Adult coloring books can also be a program in itself. The University of Nebraska at Omaha's college library runs "Color Me Calm" adult coloring book programs as a means to de-stress during college finals. They reported in a Digital Commons article that after participating the college "students seemed to leave a little bit happier," and that it helped "alleviate anxiety" about talking to librarians (Blackburn and Chamley, 2016).

Here is a sample program outline for an adapted "calming" adult coloring book activity.

SAMPLE PROGRAM IDEA: CALMING WITH COLORING

Materials:

• *Adult coloring books*. There are many different types and collections of adult coloring books. These coloring books can be expensive, so shop carefully.

Also, when purchasing look out for adult coloring books that are specifically about drawing curse words. This may or may not appropriate for your audience.

Note: Do not give out whole coloring books to participants. They may draw on several pages, smudge items, etc. People typically don't want to color on a page someone else has already started. Rip out pages from coloring books and lay them out.

- *Adult coloring sheets.* Search for copyright-free coloring sheets on Google or Pinterest to use in the program. Then simply print them out before the program.

- *Markers.* Like adult coloring books, markers can be very expensive. You may want to just use the more inexpensive Crayola or store brand markers used in other library programs, although you can also invest in a set just for this program. If you plan on repeating the adult coloring program multiple times, consider buying a set of higher-end markers. The pros of using the more expensive markers are that they don't bleed as much onto other pages, they blend well, and are easier to hold. Some brands you may consider are Faber-Castell, PrismaColor, Copic, or ColorIt ("What Are the Best Markers for Adult Coloring Books?" 2018).

- Colored pencils.

Instructions:

1. Set up tables and chairs in the room. Consider using round tables, which encourages more social interaction by everyone facing together. At each table include at least a couple of dozen markers and colored pencils.

2. Provide a variety of different colored sheets at each table and encourage participants to look around at the tables to find their favorite sheet to color. Make it clear that they can color as many sheets as they want and take them home when they are done.

3. Set out sensory items at each table as well as the coloring sheets. One idea of a calming crafting item would be playdough. Specific sensory items and how to make them will be mentioned later in this Appendix.

4. Have quiet music play in the background of the event.

5. Provide 1–2 hours of coloring time, and give 30-minute and 10-minute reminders before the program is complete.

This program can also simply be adapted as a passive program during library opening hours where the items are set out all day. If you do decide to use this as a passive program, consider not purchasing the expensive markers in case the lids are not closed and they dry out or get lost.

Optional: Provide snacks at each table while they are coloring. Put out pillows to make the chairs more comfortable. An adult coloring program can easily be an after-hours activity and last a long time. You can provide a variety of crafts along with coloring for a longer 3–4-hour activity. By having the program after the library closes, this opens up other areas to use and provides a quieter and calmer atmosphere for those with noise sensory issues.

Sensory Items

Over the years I grew my collection of sensory items that I would put out passively in my program. Some sensory activities, like slime or water play, are only used once. This section includes ideas for items that can be used again and again.

Weighted Blanket

A weighted blanket is a safe and effective way to apply weight and deep pressure, which has been found to be calming and comforting, enabling an individual to relax and go to sleep. Weighted blankets have been found to help with insomnia, autism, Asperger's, ADHD, sensory processing disorder, and others.

There are also weighted vests and other types of items that can act like a weighted blanket. In my program we had a very popular weighted snake that some of the participants would drape over their shoulders. Weighted blankets can have extra weight added to them for the size of the individual. For teens and adults with autism you will want an extra heavy blanket.

Weighted blankets can be expensive. Here are some suggestions for making your own:

- There are various items that you can use to weigh the blanket down, like aquarium stones, for example. However, through experience I would recommend Poly-Pellets. The pellets are smooth and designed for being in blankets and stuffed animals and are nontoxic and washable. The Poly-Pellets are not cheap, so consider shopping around and using a coupon.
- When creating the blanket, leave channels/columns to insert the pellets. Don't just stuff all the pellets in between the layers of the blanket, which will just make one large lump as the pellets move around the blanket. You can help make these channels with empty wrapping paper rolls. Be careful when sewing the blanket together after the pellets are through the channels because sewing needles will break if they hit the pellet.
- In general, you'll want a weighted blanket that is around 10 percent of the person's weight, or no more than 15–20 pounds (Staff, 2018).
- Convert the weight of the Poly-Pellets into ounces and divide that up into sections of the blanket. You'll want a digital scale to help make sure your measurements are correct.
- Use a durable fabric like cotton, muslin, or flannel.

Rice Box

A rice box is a fun sensory activity that can be used year-round. Make sure it's placed over a tablecloth or something to catch any spills. Rice is not the easiest to vacuum up. Do not use it near water.

To create a rice box:

1. Find a long, flat plastic bin with a lid. Consider finding one for storing items underneath beds.
2. Fill the bin with dry rice. You can also add a few bags of dry beans or peas.
3. Have the library participants mix up the rice and other dried items. It offers a certain texture and feel.
4. Every few months add more rice and/or beans into the bin. After a year empty out the contents and fill them up with fresh rice.

With the rice box you can incorporate different activities throughout the year.

- Hide fake plastic autumn leaves in the bin for the fall. You can also include other items as the seasons change: metal bells for the winter holidays, plastic hearts for Valentines, etc.
- Provide measuring cups, spoons, small shovels, and more. You can incorporate some STEM skills such as measuring by having the participants perform tasks like moving a particular measurement of rice to another bin.
- Have a sensory hunt; hide a small plastic item to be found by searching through the bin. You can also hide some clues for an activity—for example, hiding pieces of a map in the bin that need to be found and put together.

SAMPLE PROGRAM IDEA: SENSORY BOTTLES

Sensory bottles are both a potential program activity and an item you can leave out in programs as a stim/fidget toy. There are various different ways to make them. If done in an activity, let the attendees put their own creative flourishes to the toy.

Materials:

- One bottle for each participant.

  Note: There are lots of options for the bottles. You can go cheap and just find some empty water bottles. I would suggest using plastic instead of glass in case they are dropped. However, the tall glass bottles, like the brand Voss, do look very nice. You can also consider getting baby food jars for smaller sensory bottles.
- Baby oil and distilled water.

Note: When I've done this activity, I prefer baby oil. It's fairly inexpensive and found at the Dollar Store. Do not just pour regular tap water into the bottle. It has different bacteria that over time can make the sensory bottle look pretty gross. Use distilled water. You can also use canola or vegetable oil, but they have a yellow tint unlike baby oil.

- A strong glue.
- Water-based food coloring in the primary colors.

Instructions:

1. Fill half of your bottle or jar with distilled water.
2. Add two drops of the food coloring or your choice.
3. Mix the water and food coloring until it's all one color.
4. Fill up the rest of your bottle or jar with baby oil.
5. Stir the baby oil until it's blended with the food coloring.
6. This can also be a science demonstration. Have the participants pause and see what happens when they stop blending the baby oil. They will watch the oil separate from the water and float on top. You can explain that oil is less dense than water, so its upward buoyancy forces it on top of the water.
7. Use a strong glue, like super glue, to make sure the lid of the bottle or jar is secure.

Other variations on sensory bottles:

- Add glitter, lots of it, and in various sizes.
- Consider painting the outsides of the bottles.
- Include glow-in-the-dark materials like stars and beads.
- Add Jelly Beadz or other sensory/water beads to the distilled water in the bottle.
- Clear glue or hair gel and glitter can make a bottle that moves like a lava lamp.
- Put little items like small plastic toys in the bottle to add a surprise when shaking.

Sensory Items to Purchase for Programs

- *Magnet blocks.* There are different brands including Cossy Magnetic Tiles, Magna Tiles, Picasso Tiles, Magnz Wooden Bricks, and Veatree.
- *Sensory or fidget bands.* These bands are used to fidget in a program. There are different bands including ones that go on chairs that can help with fidgety feet. Ones I've used with teens successfully before are the straight, smooth, and stretchy strings about 10 inches long. The teens would wrap them around their hands and pull on them.

- *Water beads.* These are tiny hard beads that when added to water inflate for a squishy sensory experience. The brand I have used is Jelly BeadZ; one bag would last for months. Jelly BeadZ are nontoxic (Jelly BeadZ, 2020). You want to make sure you don't use water beads that are toxic when swallowed. Tapioca pearls or Popping Pearls/Boba balls are another option—which can be eaten. These are the little squishy balls added to Boba Tea or frozen yogurt. Unlike Jelly BeadZ, which can be washed with a little water and bleach and dried out, tapioca pearls can only be used once.

READING DOGS

Certified therapy animals, like reading dogs, are a furry addition to library programs for individuals with autism. A 2015 article in *Early Childhood Education Journal* states, "The use of trained therapy dogs has a long history in therapeutic and educational settings. Screened for basic obedience and a calm demeanor, these dogs provide emotional support to a variety of clients ranging from hospital patients to school children. Benefits have been reported as improvement in physiological measures, academic abilities and emotional well-being as well as reduction of stress, anxiety and loneliness" (Kirnan et al., 2016).

About once or twice a year I would invite outside partners to bring therapy animals into our library program. I had several participants over the years who had therapy dogs or emotional support animals at home. Their caregivers would tell me how appreciative they were for these animals. The dogs were a source of support through the stresses of school, therapies, and comorbid conditions. I was fortunate to have several hospitals, universities, and therapy nonprofit dogs near the library. Not all locations may have as many options. However, if your library does find a local therapy dog organization, they can be a support to programs of varying ages and abilities.

SAMPLE PROGRAM IDEA: THERAPY READING DOGS

This program is more flexible and less structured. It is similar to a passive program in which participants can choose what they want to do. Remember that not everyone likes dogs; there may be allergies or other fears, so provide alternative activities.

Materials:

- Therapy dogs. Consider getting at least one dog for every two to four participants. Ideally, each person who wants to read to a dog would have their own, but this may not be possible.
- Carpet and/or blankets. Attendees will want to get down to the level of the dog, which may require them laying on the floor.

- Selection of books to read to the dogs.
- Variety of passive activities.

Instructions:

1. *Book the therapy dogs.* Call around for a group that is available during your program. Remember that the handlers of the dogs may be volunteers and unpaid. Respect their time. If you cannot find a local group, consider calling the hospital closest to you and ask if they use therapy dogs. They may be able to direct you.

2. *Set up the room for the dogs.* Put out carpet squares, rugs, blankets, and more for them to sit on. Set out a variety of books to read to the dogs.

3. *Set out other activities for participants.* There may be only a few dogs to read to, or the attendees may not want to be close to the dogs. Some ideas for optional activities are coloring pages, blocks, sensory items, and more.

ORGANIZING AUTISM OUTREACH

The autism community is composed of many groups, organizations, individuals' agencies, and more. There are volunteers, professionals, parents, advocates, and autistics all working, but not necessarily working together. After age 21 and individuals with autism no longer can be funded through public schools, it is much more difficult to find services. This makes the community serving teens and young adults with autism even harder to navigate. Librarians need to be organized in their outreach and marketing to this population. There is not just one place or person to reach out to. Information is not always disseminated to the people who need to see it. A professional in one agency might not be aware of what's happening across town.

In Chapters 4 and 6 you can read more tips to marketing to teens and adults with autism. Included are suggestions to specifically target your outreach.

To stay organized with your library's partnerships in autism, see Table A.1, a sample template to track and follow up with outreach.

TABLE A.1. Sample Template of Outreach Tracker

Date	Person/ Organization Contacted	Title	Contact Info	Concerning	Contacted by whom?	Follow up
2/8/2020	Smith County School District	Transition Specialist	Jane Doe 555-555-5555 jdoe@ smithcounty.org	Autism Teen Library Program	Carrie	Will call in two weeks

In addition to a tracking sheet, here are other suggestions to create and maintain those valuable relationships in the autism community:

- Create the outreach tracker on a shared drive if you are working with multiple people. Set permissions so everyone can add to the tracker. It looks unprofessional and causes confusion if multiple people from the library contact the same organization and/or person. A shared spreadsheet also creates better accountability with your staff members. You know what they've committed to do and can make sure they follow through.

- If you receive a business card from someone, write a note on the back with a personal detail. It can be hard to remember everyone if you're at an outreach or networking event. If you write a simple comment like "Knows this branch manager," "Tall, black-haired," or "Starting new program in fall," that can jump-start your memory and help with follow through.

- Another way to organize business cards is through an app. Apps that scan and automatically add the person's info to your e-mail client include CamCard, Wantedly People, Microsoft Office Lens, and CardHQ (free).

- Set digital reminders. In addition to using the outreach tracking sheet, set your own digital reminders on your calendar. Set an alarm or reminder to go off every other Friday, or another time where you may have less work during the day. That can remind you to check in on those networks, autism communication, and more.

REFERENCES

Admin. 2019, November 8. "13 DIY Mini Zen Garden Ideas for Desk." Balcony Garden Web. https://balconygardenweb.com/diy-mini-zen-garden-ideas-for -desk.

Blackburn, Heidi, and Claire E. Chamley. 2016. "Color Me Calm: Adult Coloring and the University Library." *Criss Library Faculty Proceedings & Presentations* 78. https://digitalcommons.unomaha.edu/crisslibfacproc/78.

Bulnick, Penolopy. "Robot Costumes." Instructables. Accessed February 7, 2020. https://www.instructables.com/id/Robot-Costumes.

"Contact Jim." Jim Gill—Music Play for All Young Children. Accessed February 7, 2020. https://jimgill.com.

Dann, Christina. 2016, February 1. "Tissue Paper Wreath Tutorial." A Blissful Nest. https://ablissfulnest.com/tissue-paper-wreath-tutorial.

"Educational Kits." Educational Kits. 4-H. Accessed February 7, 2020. https://shop4 -h.org/collections/educational-kits.

"GIMP." GIMP. Accessed February 7, 2020. https://www.gimp.org.

"Jelly BeadZ Inc.—Water Beads, Vase Fillers, Water Beads for Plants." JellyBeadZ. Accessed February 7, 2020. http://www.jellybeadz.com.

Kirnan, Jean, Steven Siminerio, and Zachary Wong. 2016. "The Impact of a Therapy Dog Program on Children's Reading Skills and Attitudes toward Reading." *Early Childhood Education Journal* 44, no. 6: 637–51. doi:10.1007/s10643- 015-0747-9.

Rogers-Whitehead, Carrie. 2015, May 12. "7 Easy STEM Activities You Can Do at Home." KSL.com. KSL. https://www.ksl.com/article/34603810/7-easy-stem-activities-you-can-do-at-home.

Rogers-Whitehead, Carrie. 2016, November 29. "5 STEM Activities You Can Do at Home with 6 Supplies or Less." KSL.com. https://www.ksl.com/article/42388315/5-stem-activities-you-can-do-at-home-with-6-supplies-or-less.

Rogers-Whitehead, Carrie. 2017, May 31. "4 Geeky Activities to Get Your Child Interested in STEM." KSL. https://www.ksl.com/article/44462005/4-geeky-activities-to-get-your-child-interested-in-stem.

Rogers-Whitehead, Carrie. 2018. *Teen Fandom and Geek Programming: A Practical Guide for Librarians*. Lanham, MD: Rowman & Littlefield.

Staff, WikiHow. 2019, September 6. "How to Make a Weighted Blanket." wikiHow. https://www.wikihow.com/Make-a-Weighted-Blanket.

"StoryBots." StoryBots. Accessed February 7, 2020. https://www.storybots.com.

"Teaching Toolboxes." 2019, November 19. Natural History Museum of Utah. https://nhmu.utah.edu/educators/teaching-toolboxes.

Thompson, William Forde, and Gottfried Schlaug. 2015. "The Healing Power of Music." *Scientific American Mind* 26, no. 2: 32. doi:10.1038/scientificamericanmind0315-32.

Twarogowski, Tricia. 2009, June 23. "Programming for Children with Special Needs, Part One." ALSC Blog, Association for Library Service to Children. https://www.alsc.ala.org/blog/2009/06/programming-for-children-with-special-needs-part-one.

"What Are the Best Markers for Adult Coloring Books?" 2018, May 23. ColorIt. https://www.colorit.com/blogs/news/what-are-the-best-markers-for-adult-coloring-books.

Index

About the Author

CARRIE ROGERS-WHITEHEAD, MLIS, MPA, is the founder of Digital Respons-Ability and has worked in libraries for over a decade. Through her library work she created the first sensory program in the state of Utah for individuals with autism and received the Utah Librarian of the Year Award for that work. Carrie regularly trains and consults librarians and continues her work with individuals with autism with Digital Respons-Ability. She is the author of *Digital Citizenship: Teaching Strategies and Practice from the Field*, *Teen Fandom and Geek Programming: A Practical Guide for Librarians*, and the upcoming title *Becoming a Digital Parent*.